Equipping Spirit-Led Leaders

Empowering Current and Potential Leaders for Kingdom Service

by Dr. I. Franklin Perkins

dpRochelle
**PO Box 9523
Hampton, Virginia 23670
1 (757) 825-0030
ItsmeDrIFP.org**

© 2015 Dr. I. Franklin Perkins. All Rights Reserved

No part of this book may be reproduced, stored in a retrieval system, or transmitted by any means without the written permission of the author.

First published by dpRochelle 3/9/15
Second Edition published by dpRochelle 6/1/16

ISBN: 978-0-9862389-2-5

Printed in the United States of America, Hampton, Virginia

DEDICATION

Dedicated to those who are faced with leadership anxiety.

". . . knowing things causes you to see problems everywhere. If, however, you are willfully stupid, you can keep doing things the same way."[1]

    Herb Miller

---

[1] Herb Miller, *Leadership is the Key: Unlocking Your Ministry Effectiveness* (Abingdon Press, Nashville, TN 1997), 13.

TABLE OF CONTENTS

1	Chapter 1	Leadership Foundations
11	Chapter 2	Leading by Understanding Spiritual Gifts
		a. Manifestation Gifts
		b. Ministry (Administration) Gifts
		c. Motivational (Operation) Gifts
55	Chapter 3	Leadership Roles in the Church
		a. Pastor, (Bishop, Overseer, Elder)
		b. Deacon
85	Chapter 4	Leading Effectively
		a. Prayer
		b. How to Deal with Conflict
107	Chapter 5	Leadership Field Experience
127	Chapter 6	Learning of Recommended Reading
135	Chapter 7	Leadership Research of General Reflections
137	Bibliography	
149	Appendices A - C	
		Leadership Survey for Pastors
		Sample Organizational Charts
		Congregational Care Organizational Chart
	Workbook	

Foreword by Stephen Swisher

It is indeed my pleasure to endorse this exciting new work from Dr. I. Franklin Perkins. I have known her personally for more than seven years and have watched her as pastor, musician, motivational speaker and Church leadership expert. This new work began as a doctoral project and has grown to a vital resource for pastors, Church lay leaders and anyone interested in developing their skill sets to maximize their potential for the Lord Jesus Christ.

This is a valuable resource and a must read for anyone involved in ministry or the work of the Church. Especially those who want to discover, understand and employ leadership tools in a complex and often confusing world.

Dr. Perkins is an expert in the area of Church administration and effective leadership. I encourage you to use this resource as a manual to be read and re-read and returned to on a frequent basis. Dog ear your favorite parts and let the research, heart and talent of Dr. Perkins aid you in going to the next level of successful mission and ministry.

God bless you on the journey.

Rev. Dr. Stephen Swisher
Senior Pastor, Epiphany United Methodist Church, Cincinnati;
President, Swisher Evangelistic Association, Inc.,
Former Senior Executive, Kenneth Copeland Ministries
 and Director of Kenneth Copeland Scholars

Preface

After years of observing local churches, I have come to the conclusion that leaders rarely understand what to do in their particular leadership roles. The governance of the church is often placed in the hands of those that are not qualified to handle positions of authority and therefore lack effectiveness. This causes a trickle-down effect of repetitive dissonance and ill-managed delegation for those who serve in the reporting chain of the assumed leader. There is a needed shift from leadership mediocrity to quality leadership in the church. The current leadership needs to be rejuvenated and the potential leaders need to be empowered in the context by understanding the spiritual gifts that they possess, understanding how to utilize their discovered gift(s), understanding which leadership style influences their decision base, realizing the importance of identifying leadership roles in the church, and understanding how to lead effectively through prayer and conflict resolution.

It is to this end that a consolidated paradigm was developed to enable those in this context to be adequately refined for Kingdom service. The information proposed is devised to cultivate individuals and small groups for leadership advantages. It is with intent that I introduce current and potential leaders to coaching that would improve their understanding in the above subject matter. By introducing this instructional material, it will empower current and potential leaders for Kingdom service.

ACKNOWLEDGMENTS

To my husband Pastor Dr. Derrick, Sr. and our children, Dee, Jr. and Aegious who have so graciously supported all of my endeavors, even though, my time was always confiscated by the cares of everything else. I ultimately thank God for the strength to endure and the ability to reason.

Special Thanks To:

Patricia A. Johnson
Rev. Luther S. Allen, III
Dr. Angela D. Washington - Dr. Donnell J. Moore
Dr. Leroy Cothran - Dr. Reginald Dawkins
Dr. Howard E. Heard - Dr. Arnita Snead Brooks

INTRODUCTION

Equipping Spirit-Led Leaders began as a work to train leaders in the church to lead others effectively. However it developed into a model to enhance the knowledge base of current and potential leaders relating to leadership roles in the church, self-development and character building in a leadership capacity.

Often, leaders move on to other ministry obligations, which can cause a surge in assumed control by unqualified personnel who may not have the skill set nor the basic understanding of leadership concepts. Some leaders are challenged by differences in the viewpoint of the church's atmosphere but ongoing guidance from advisors who will hold them accountable will provide steady counsel to empower leaders to impact ministry. Due to cultural changes it is necessary to revisit leadership abilities to circumvent a "crash and burn" demise in the church. It is to this end, that leaders should understand how to utilize their spiritual gifts, acknowledge leadership roles in the church and how to effectively lead through prayer and conflict resolution.

The purpose of this book is to discuss a coaching platform that will empower current and potential leaders for Kingdom service. Empower is defined in this context as an improvement in the overall understanding of an individual as it relates to the subject matter of leadership and its components. Leaders in this setting are defined as those who have or have had a minimum of one person reporting to them in a church setting or those who make decisions that will affect others. Potential leaders from this perspective are defined as those who may or may not have exemplified the ability to lead others in a church setting. While

Kingdom service in this framework is defined as the system of God, which operates in a supernatural manner through a natural manifestation.

It is presupposed that if relevant information is communicated that addresses organizational leadership through understanding spiritual gifts, leadership roles in the church, and how to effectively lead through prayer and conflict resolution, it will empower current and potential leaders for leadership.

Equipping Spirit-Led Leaders

Empowering Current and Potential Leaders for Kingdom Service

by Dr. I. Franklin Perkins

Chapter 1
Leadership Foundations

Over the years, church has evolved yet remained the same based on the following comments relating to church leadership which are rather daunting but true. In his book, *Spiritual Leadership in a Secular Age,* Edward Hammett writes, "My church is stuck because some of the leadership refuses to consider any changes that are uncomfortable for them, declared a frustrated pastor. Until Mr. B- dies, our church will never be able to make any changes, explained a church leader. How does a church avoid conflict in dealing with respected, long-time members who are often a barrier to growth and progress? Questioned a faithful leader."[2] Regrettably, many churches all over the world have experienced uncompromising leaders and also a Mr. B- in the congregation who likes things just the way they are, even though, they may sometimes hinder progress.

In addition, Hammett writes, "My leaders are crying for training, but they will not attend training meetings. What am I to do, asked a frustrated church leader? My leaders are not committed to the tasks at hand. They are unmotivated and seemingly unconcerned about the church's programming. How can I move my leaders from just wanting to talk about things to getting around to doing something that needs to be done, exclaimed a senior pastor?"[3] The avoidance of training will also stunt the growth of a ministry.

---

[2]Edward H. Hammett, *Spiritual Leadership in a Secular Age: Building Bridges Instead of Barriers* (St. Louis, MO: Chalice Press, 2005), 147.

[3]Ibid., 136.

These comments and many other comments like these were stated by pastors and senior leaders from various areas of ministry. Leadership is one of the key essentials in helping individuals to become all that God wants them to become. In fact, the Bible tells us, "Without wise leadership, a nation falls; there is safety in having many advisers," (Prv 11:14-NLT). Therefore, leadership is necessary to families, businesses, communities, churches and the world, for without it, trouble is imminent. In his book, *Be the Leader You Were Meant to Be,* Leroy Eims says that leaders are the first ones who can see things before others do, respond to situations quicker than others and has foresight to know what is on the horizon. Leaders map out directions for others to follow as a result of their anticipation.[4] There is a spiritual focus unique to the Kingdom of God that undergirds the desire to revolutionize and empower leaders for a successful outcome while leading others. As leadership evolves, the process will have a considerable effect on the church at large. As Gene Mims writes in *The Kingdom-Focused Church,* "We desperately need pastors and church leaders who understand what a church is and who are willing to work to see that their churches become what God desires: churches with a Kingdom-focus above everything else." When the purpose of the church becomes the heart of God, then great things will begin to happen. A church that is Kingdom-focused is one that is modest, simplified, and exhilarating. Often, current leaders are neither forward thinkers nor are they ready to advance with a Kingdom focus because of sedentary

---

[4]Leroy Eims, *Be the Leader You Were Meant to Be: Biblical Principles of Leadership* (Wheaton, IL: Victor Books, 1977), 20.

behavior. However, results can still be achieved if the leader takes a small group of potentials, toward a Kingdom focus.[5]

Leadership is necessary to assist people in achieving excellence and flexibility as one stays on the cutting edge of revolutionary change. This encourages a leader to have the opportunity to explore unpaved routes of thought, which will transcend beyond the in-box structure. Warren Bennis writes, "Leadership is a function of knowing yourself, having a vision that is well-communicated, building trust among colleagues, and taking effective action to realize your own leadership potential."[6] This process will cultivate a more fruitful response from those who are involved.

Leaders are those who can develop, lead, mentor, train and commission other individuals as well as cultivate their gifts and talents for service for the Kingdom. This will raise "leaders who will finish well, leaders who will lead well, and leaders who will leave a legacy of transformed lives because of the way they communicate the heart of God and their own hearts to those they are raising."[7] Leadership is reinventing quality leaders for a lifetime.

Terry Thomas writes, "When the people we lead express statements of discontentment because of facing what appears to be insurmountable challenge,

---

[5]Gene Mims, *The Kingdom-Focused Church* (Nashville, TN: Broadman & Homan Publishers, 2003), 175.

[6]Warren Bennis, *The Leadership Advantage: Leader to Leader* (New York, NY, Spring 1999), 18-23.

[7]Dr. Joseph Umidi, *Transformational Coaching: Bridge Building that Impacts, Connects, and Advances the Ministry and the Marketplace* (Maitland, FL, Xulon Press, 2005), 32.

we must respond to them with a message of hope, an extreme confidence in God's ability to handle the situation." This does not suggest that the leader gives hope based on their abilities to lead but to point the people towards the One who is hope. Thomas writes, "the manner in which a person responds to the initial statement of discontentment is a means in which a person's leadership begins to be established in the eyes of the people he or she has been appointed to lead." A leader will redirect the attention to what is really important.[8]

So, exactly what is leadership? It is influence. If a person can influence another, then this makes them a leader. A person who desires to influence others for the benefit of others becomes the primary influencer who realizes that it is not who he or she is but rather the ability of empowering others to be transformed. Leaders can influence others in good ways as well as not so good ways. However, God expects His Church to influence the world according to His purpose instead of the world influencing the church. This definition is pointed directly towards the potential of the individual leader.[9]

A similar response of leadership is given in the book *Spiritual Leadership*, where J. Oswald Sanders writes that, "Leadership is influence. I have embraced that definition and taught it to thousands and thousands over the years. If you are a follower of Christ, then you recognize that you are called to influence others. Jesus said it this way: "You are the salt of the earth. . . You are the light of the

---

[8]Terry Thomas, *An Exploration into the Task of Leadership* (lecture notes from cluster group/Handout), 43.

[9]Deepak Chopra, *The Soul of Leadership* (New York, NY: Harmony Books, 2010), 9.

world. . . Let your light so shine before men, that they may see your good works and glorify your Father in heaven" (Mt 5:13-16).[10] J. Oswald Sanders further writes, "It doesn't matter if you are a CEO or a stay-at-home mom; if you call yourself a Christian, then you are called to influence others. That's why it's important for you to learn to become a better leader—whether you are the parent in a family, the pastor of a church, the president of a company, or a potential leader for the next generation." Christian leaders are called to influence the world.[11]

However, the influence of others does not always stand on its own bottom. John C. Maxwell writes, "Influence by itself is not enough. That influence must be measured to determine its *quality*." It is necessary to find out "who influences the leader" and "whom does the leader influence?" These factors are vital to the end result of influence. It is imperative to know the type of inspiration that a leader receives, especially if there is an option to choose the best current and/or potential leader.[12]

In the sermon, *The Skills of Leadership, Part 3,* Pastor William D. Tyree, III, writes, "One of the greatest myths about leadership is that leaders are born. They are *not* born. Leaders are made. Some people think, 'I was born a leader,' or 'I am not born a leader.' And that is it. No, no! Leaders are made by two things.

---

[10]J. Oswald Sanders, *Spiritual Leadership,* Revised Edition (Chicago, IL: Moody Bible Institute, 1980), 10.

[11]Ibid., 10.

[12]John C. Maxwell, *Developing the Leaders Around You* (Nashville, TN: INVOY, Inc. 1995), 49.

They are made by choices, and they are made by circumstances. When you make the right choices in the right circumstances you too can be a great leader." Although some are born with the gift of administration and the grace to lead (Chapter 2), it is to be understood that quality leadership can be determined by the choices made by an individual.[13]

In the book, *The Soul of Leadership,* Deepak Chopra opens Chapter 1 of his book, with a life-changing quote, "Becoming a leader is the most crucial choice one can make-it is the decision to step out of darkness into the light." It is the decision of the individual to be willing to move from obscurity to illumination.[14] Therefore, when change is implemented in the church from a traditional culture of ungodly rituals and religious patterns, positive transformative processes could bring resistance to the change. Those who are comfortable with the normalcy of a structure that does not evolve may not be able to grasp the concept of reorganization and maintaining organizational structure nor see the need to institutionalize organizational leadership in the church. Edward Hammett expressed an enlightening moment he experienced as it relates to challenges of culture transformation. Hammett writes, ". . . I was privileged to watch the fog begin to lift amidst the beautiful sunrise, with the dew glistening . . . It was an ah hah moment for me. It was as if God said, 'When the blanket of fog lifts from our churches, they will see all the beauty underneath. They will see my

---

[13]William D. Tyree, III, *The Skills of Leadership*, Part 3 (Sermon preached at 1st Baptist Church Berkley in Norfolk on 25 October 2005).

[14]Chopra, 9.

creation, the beauty of the mission field I have planted them in for the purpose of service.'" The church is blinded by spiritual fog that keeps its members bound in the rudiments of tradition and religion. When uncomely practices are recognized in the church, it is necessary for leaders to restructure with a biblical focus in mind without fear of retribution.[15]

Hammett also writes, "In each chapter you will find coaching questions to help leaders begin to work with what often seems like overwhelming fog and often disturbing realities of a new culture. The coaching questions are designed to help you move from where you are to where God wants you to go. The coaching questions will also provide focus and intentional plans for forward movement and action." It seems that the church shows a lack of vision with regard to seeing the full purpose that God has for His people which will require the church to grab hold to transformation.[16]

Historically, many professionals who investigate leadership have tried to describe the concept as they research the character of leaders. This is a development of evolution in leadership history. The study of leadership finds its origin in the beginning of our civilization. From kings, biblical patriarchs and historical heroes there has been one consistency—leadership. "Our work environment, worker motivations, leaders, managers, and leadership styles, have been studied for almost two centuries. Over time, organizations have evolved from those with an authoritarian style to ones with a more comfortable work

---

[15]Hammett, 4.

[16]Ibid., 4.

environment, and then to organizations where people are empowered, encouraged, and supported in their personal and professional growth."[17] Although there may be many theories and classifications of leadership, J. T. Wren asserts that the definition for leadership even in the beginning of civilization meant influence and power to induce compliance. Leader-focus has transitioned over time, and also the nuances of leader-focus as captured in the progression of leadership theory.[18] As leadership theory advances, we may struggle with the process of developing individuals who may feel inadequate for any position. What do people do to improve when they are left to their own resources and do not know how to improve? In recent years it has been observed that leaders, who are left without training in the areas of understanding spiritual gifts, leadership roles in the church, and how to effectively lead, may suffer many social and relational challenges as they attempt to lead others. Many times you will find that leaders are only concerned with the "back then" and the "right now" with little regard to the "later on." Consequently, long-term leaders may feel entitled to the position they hold rather than a need to empower up-and-coming leaders who may become stunted from a lack of encouragement from their predecessors. When empowerment is not the intent, this causes current and potential leaders to cease from growing towards their potential which can ultimately cripple a church. Edward Hammett explains how entitlement not only plagues those in leadership but also spills over into the

---

[17]J. T. Wren, *The Leaders Companion: Insights on Leadership Through the Ages* (New York, NY: The Free Press, 1995).

[18]Ibid.

church as a whole therein leaving poisonous deposits. He writes, "Spiritual leadership as the church involves reframing church, reframing leadership, and reframing the journey. . . Unfortunately, routine has become the norm for many church leaders. . . Most church leaders these days have an entitlement mentality. This leads them to value a stable system rather than venture out on an empowerment objective."[19] Sadly, the entitlement mindset stops the possibility of potential leaders becoming what God has purposed for their lives. This could lead to a shortage of quality leadership in many settings. However, the training of organizational leadership including understanding spiritual gifts, leadership roles in the church, and how to effectively lead is a necessary format for empowerment. If current and potential leaders choose this option, entitlement will no longer be the norm.

Leaders who welcome the empowerment of the Holy Spirit open themselves to an atmosphere that is conducive for giving birth to higher levels of innovation. However, when the personal comforts of individuals become the priority, the desire for entitlement dampens the movement of the Holy Spirit. Hammett continues to write, "Empowerment releases - Entitlement controls; Empowerment creates - Entitlement kills; Empowerment is about His mission - Entitlement is about our agendas."[20] This is so often the case in many settings which is considered inevitable death for those who deny the need for change. Let us take a look at a few factors that gives segue to empowering potential leaders.

---

[19]Hammett, 148.

[20]Ibid., 150.

First, leaders must understand their spiritual gifts. The Scripture identifies three categories of gifts: manifestation gifts, ministry (administration) gifts and motivational (operation) gifts.[21] The Scripture further identifies at least three ways that will enhance the utilization of these gifts which are through: maturity, unity and love (Eph 4:14).

Secondly, leaders should understand leadership roles in their particular church. In the Old Testament the leadership roles were the priest and the prophet. In the New Testament the leadership roles in the church were apostle, evangelist, pastor (bishop, elder and overseer were used synonymously with pastor) and deacon.

Thirdly, leaders must understand how to effectively lead in order to make impact for the Kingdom. Two of the ways to lead effectively are through prayer and conflict resolution.

The lack of effective leadership in the church is a growing concern because it not only damages the credibility of ministry but it also infringes upon the ability for the church to activate successfully in its mission of discipleship. Of course, these findings are not a cure-all but it will be a reasonable place to start to encourage a brighter future for our churches by *Equipping Spirit-Led Leaders and Empowering Current and Potential Leaders for Kingdom Service.*

---

[21] Don and Kate Fortune. *Discover Your God-Given Gifts* (Grand Rapids, MI: Chosen Books, a division of Baker Book House Company, 1987), 17.

Chapter 2

Leading by Understanding Spiritual Gifts

An individual has all the characteristics, skills and abilities within themselves in order to be the leader that God has called them to be. The champion is lying dormant inside just waiting to excel in the area best suited for them. Michael Scott writes,

> …there is a champion on the inside of you waiting to be released. You are not a loser, you are a leader. You may have been hindered or held back by certain life circumstances, but you can no longer afford to allow the champion spirit to lie dormant within. You have been bringing in the rear long enough. You have been on the listening and observing end of the spectrum for far too long. It is now your time to make significant strides in your respective field that will impact your surrounding community, your nation, and your world for the Christ within you. A champion is one that exemplifies the meaning of superiority. Michael Jordan is an NBA champion because of superior skills in basketball. Tiger Woods is a PGA champion because of his superior skills and abilities in golf. And yes, you are a champion because of your superior characteristics and abilities that are waiting to be fully released into this world so that others may benefit from your leadership.[22]

Many do not believe that spiritual gifts are even necessary to accomplish the mission of the church and feel that they have little to do with the effects of

---

[22] Michael Thomas Scott, *The Leader Within* (Temperanceville, VA: Rhema Word Publishing, 2005), 119.

leadership. In the book *Missional Church: A Vision for the Sending of the Church in North America* by Darrell L. Guder, he writes, "The Spirit empowers the church for mission through the gifts of people." There is a need for God-revived leadership if there will be a change in our regions. Guder further writes, "Such leadership will be biblically and theologically astute, skilled in understanding the changes shaping North American society, and gifted with the courage and endurance to lead God's people as missional communities." The leader has a responsibility to initiate change in the community by using their God-given ability. Scriptures establish that to bring basic modifications to a group of individuals necessitates leaders who are skilled and gifted in initiating variations that will not only revolutionize the group but also themselves in the process.

Therefore, "leadership is a critical gift, provided by the Spirit."[23] It is necessary to activate this gift to be of service to others. Paul tells Timothy to stir up the gift of God which is already inside him because Paul laid hands on him to receive the Holy Spirit (2 Tim 1:6); Timothy had the responsibility to metaphorically fan (or stir up – anazopureo) the flame of the Holy Spirit to rekindle this gift by reason of use. When a leader is chosen and consecrated for spiritual service, it is an assignment for the life of the individual which cannot be revoked as the "gifts and calling of God are without repentance (Ro 11:29). This passage expresses that God will never change His mind concerning the gifts *(charisma)* or calling *(klesis)* that He has bestowed upon His people even if we never use them; they are a part of us forever. God tells Jeremiah, "Before I

---

[23]Darrell L. Guder, *Missional Church: A Vision for the Sending of the Church in North America.* (Grand Rapids, MI: William B. Eerdmans Publishing Company, 1998), 183.

formed you in the womb I knew you, before you were born I set you apart; I appointed you as a prophet to the nations" (Jer 1:5). God designated our gifts and callings long before we were born and knitted our purpose into our DNA (Psa 139:13).

It is to this end that every person was created with a gift, and will always have something specific that they can do. In *Developing the Leaders Around You,* John C. Maxwell writes, "Every person God creates has gifts. One of our jobs as leaders is to make an assessment of those gifts when considering a person for employment." Then Maxwell lists what he calls the four types of wanna bes, which is a description of the different levels of employees and their abilities.

The first level employee is: The "Never be"—which is a person who has gifts and abilities but not for the job that they have been assigned to do. They may continue on this inappropriate track for many years, however complaining all the way until they retire. Unfortunately they come up short in results and then "often blame others" for their frustrations and failure to succeed. The frustrations of their failure often foster a negative attitude and a hostile environment around the "Never be" which can cause colleague isolation and no consideration for promotion. The possible fix would be a reassignment to the appropriate task which would be an attempt to resolve the challenge and may increase productivity. However, this person would be difficult to develop without consistent one on one coaching and training.[24]

---

[24]Maxwell, 52.

The next level employee is, The "Could be"—which is a person who has gifts and abilities but does not have the self-discipline to maintain his or her obligations. They have the wherewithal to get the job done but are satisfied with where they are; they tend to do just enough to get by and deliberately fly under the radar to avoid detection. Promotion is possible but often declined as it will require the "Could be" to come out of their comfort zone. This person would need to practice self-control and reroute their focus to prevent being blindsided by personal and social pressures. The possibility of evolving to the next level would require training and consistent follow-up for this person, otherwise they could fall into the slumps of the "Never-be" employee.[25]

The next level employee is, The "Should be"—which is a person who has the gifts that are necessary, actual raw talent, but does not possess the knowledge and skill sets to cultivate the abilities. Often, they may experience a few "hit or miss" successes due to the inability to make appropriate decisions based on their limited comprehension of seeing the whole picture. This person will rely on what they have experienced which may no longer be relevant to the task at hand. Promotion is certain but may be on a temporary basis. This employee would benefit from leadership mentoring and seeking after higher education to perfect their trade. This will help the individual to improve overall and have an impactful outcome.[26]

---

[25]Ibid.

[26]Ibid.

The next level employee is, The "Must be"—which is a person who has the gifts, talents, knowledge, skill sets, abilities and a positive attitude but is not offered opportunity to utilize the above. While taking advantage of every opportunity to hone their craft, this person surpasses their counterparts because they are hungry and not satisfied with the status quo. They are often overlooked by their leaders who may feel inferior to their gifts yet the exceptional work that they do is always noticed by others. Their personal drive supersedes the drive of those around them because they have a clear focus and are not afraid to take a risk. They are innovative and driven to flourish by any means necessary. If this person is not afforded an opportunity within their immediate organization they will eventually find opportunity elsewhere and soar far beyond where they were.[27]

These findings are seen in various areas of secular settings as well as ministry settings because they both involve people who transfer their gifts, knowledge, skills and abilities from one venue to another, many times without much deviation. Although ministry settings offer volunteer positions, these levels of employees are present, nonetheless.

In *Organizing Genius: The Secrets of Creative Collaboration,* Warren Bennis and Patricia Ward Biederman analyze leadership by saying that leaders who are insecure about themselves and lack the ability to appreciate variety will typically recruit people who are just like themselves without realizing that the absence of diversity cripples an organization. On the other hand, there is a better type of leader, "who realizes you can only accomplish extraordinary things by

---

[27]Ibid., 53.

involving excellent people who can do things that you cannot."[28] The latter type of leader will be the successful leader as the gifts of others are a contribution to the task.

In the secular world of business organization, managers and leaders are responsible overall for the failures as well as the successes of a company. If there is anything that goes wrong with costs, inventory, overages, unexpected challenges, the management is to be held accountable for the best or the worst of times. However they are in the right position to make a positive impact for the betterment of the company and remove the 'deadly diseases' which causes the ineffectiveness of an organization.[29] In order to be an empowered leader for Kingdom service, it is necessary for the leaders of the church to accept the responsibility to equip the people for ministry. God calls all leaders to accountability (Gen 9-17).

Historically, there is significance for each Christian to "participate in the life of a local church with the gifts(s) God has given him or her." It is purposed that others will be edified through their service to one another (1 Cor 12:1-31). One who claims Christianity would be considered sinning if they are not sharing

---

[28] Warren Bennis and Patricia Ward Biederman, *Organizing Genius: The Secret of Creative Collaboration* (New York, NY: Basic Books, A member of the Perseus Books Group, 1997), 89.

[29] James L. Gibson, John M. Ivancevich, James H. Donnelly, Jr. *Organizations: Behavior, Structure, Processes,* (Burr Ridge, IL: Irwin, 8th ed.), 22.

themselves with their Christian brothers and sisters in order to edify the body of Christ as a member of the body (1 Cor 12:7; 14:6; 12, 26b).[30]

In his book, *Calvin and the Spiritual Gifts,* Paul Elbert conveys a message of instruction for each one who has received a gift (*charisma*). He stresses the importance of employing the gifts in serving others as "good stewards of the manifold grace of God," (1 Pt 4:10). He understands that we become less than productive when we withhold what is meant to be shared abroad. We must realize that God has entrusted us with a fragment of Himself through special gifts to use on this condition: "that they are applied to the common good of the church. And therefore the lawful use of all benefits consists in a liberal and kindly sharing of them with others." Our neighbors are the recipients of our endowments. As each person activates their gift, it is good to remember that the benefits of use far outweigh the penalties of holding on to what is non-productive until disbursed for the greater good.[31]

In *Understanding Leadership,* Tom Marshall writes six key factors that will assist in understanding the character of the distinct gifts.[32]

1. Each person has his own uniqueness. 'God is the Creator, and the mark of creativity is always originality; therefore, each human being in the mix of his or her God-given strengths and interests is unique and inimitable.' Because each person is different no one should compare themselves to another person. They should not be 'measured against

---

[30] Mark Driscoll, *On Church Leadership* (Crossway Books, 2008), 12.

[31] Paul Elbert, *Calvin and the Spiritual Gifts* (JETS 22/3 September 1979), 238.

[32] Tom Marshall, *Understanding Leadership* (Grand Rapids, MI: Baker Books, 2003), 188.

statistical averages' nor categorized in various groups of study.[33]

2. God's thumbprint on the life of the individual is the gift in which He gives to them to use. Each gift is designed to work appropriately when invoked. The Bible says that 'God makes even the wrath of man to praise Him' which is why no one can be successful in any endeavor without using their God-given gift. No one could sing, dance, cook a full course meal, teach or lay bricks without operating in a gift that God has given. In other words, there will be no effectiveness in any vocation unless the gifts from God are used. They are necessary in every aspect of life.[34]

3. God made humankind with a specific purpose in mind to His intended design. The intention of the Creator will enable the creature 'to fulfill a purpose.' Because this is the case, 'we have been equipped by God with the capacity to be good at some things but not good at everything, to excel at some tasks but not at every task.' It is believed that people who are accomplished discover their gifts and spend time honing their craft in order to capitalize on their specialty versus discovering their strengths then working on their weaknesses.[35]

4. The gifts given to each individual by God not only bring the individuals a sense of delight, gratification and satisfaction but they also allow them to effectively perform at maximum capacity. When the gifts are activated and

---

[33]Ibid.

[34]Ibid.

[35]Ibid.

used within the purpose for which they are intended an individual receives gratification and contributes toward productivity and produces good work in the process. Interestingly enough, the specified gifts are desired and need little prodding to be used and actually bring a sigh of relief when the individual is able to use what is already a part of them. It is always a joy to use them and never a boring obligation when operating within purpose. They work with little thought. The ability of the person gives an inner peace to the owner and serves as basically par for the course.[36]

5. 'A person's strengths and interests are gifts.' Gifts are just that, gifts. One cannot work to receive them nor can they be bought; the Creator gives them. To this end, it is the Creator to whom the person must provide accountability for the use or mismanagement of the gift. It is the obligation of the individual to be a good steward over the gifts given to receive an ultimate desired outcome.[37]

6. The impartation of God-given gifts is automatically a part of an individual's being from the beginning of time. The inspirations are 'innate behavior' and will not veer from the script for the duration of the lifetime of the person. "He will use the abilities with greater degrees of competency and complexity as he matures, but the pattern of strengths remains consistent throughout the whole life span. It follows that if we discover a person's pattern of abilities, we have something that is highly predictive. If in the past he functioned most effectively and most harmoniously within a certain range of abilities, we know that he will

---

[36]Ibid., 188-189.

[37]Ibid.

always function best when he is using those same capacities. The motivated abilities pattern, therefore, becomes the key to the most effective use of human resources, both in terms of productivity and in terms of fulfillment." When an individual enjoys what they believe is their purpose and operates in their function that is when productivity is reached. However, aggravation and irritation develop when productivity has not been achieved or gift discovered.[38]

Each person should use whatever gift they have received to serve others as faithful stewards of God's grace in its various forms (1 Pt 4:10). Don and Kate Fortune take a simple approach to the attributes and identification of spiritual gifts. They effectively address the gifts in specific groups namely; manifestation, 1 Corinthians 12:8-11; ministry (administration), Ephesians 4:11-16 and motivational (operation) gifts Romans 12:4-10; respectively.[39] In order to live a life with purpose and to perform at the maximum capacity of leadership, one should identify his or her specific gifts. God does not want us to be ignorant of the things concerning spiritual gifts (1 Cor 12:1) but that we would activate them and understand that there are many gifts but all are birthed through one Spirit.

It is necessary to mention that the gifts are still in action. There has been a question over the ages whether or not spiritual gifts still exist or, "Did they cease with the closing of Scripture at the end of the apostolic age?" Depending on the interpretation of the Scriptures, one could defend this question either way. Glen

---

[38]Ibid.

[39]Fortune, *Discover Your God-Given Gifts*...15.

Hinson mentions in his article, *The Significance of Glossolalia in the History of Christianity*, that if "the individual facts are viewed in isolation you may find ammunition to support both points of view." However, if historical evidence as a whole is looked at the outcome will be that tongues have been neither as significant as Pentecostals claim or as insignificant or as bad as some non-Pentecostals claim.[40] The Pentecostals desire was to prove that the tongues and charismatic gifts were in full affect throughout the first century only to find out that the gifts actually continued throughout the first several centuries. This finding points to such movements as Montanism as an example of God's continuation of these gifts. They assert that the decline of these gifts was a sure sign that the Church had abandoned its original fervor and succumbed to pagan influences in theology and liturgy.[41]

On the opposite end of the debate, Phillip Schaff, a historian from the 19th century felt that, "Tongues passed away gradually with the extraordinary or strictly miraculous gifts." Others, such as B. B. Warfield, refer to testimony of history and that miracles accordingly ceased with the apostolic age, and only after an interval are heard again. Even though some of the Church Fathers, Justin Martyr, Tertullian, Irenaeus, and Ambrose make mention of the gifts of tongues and prophecy long after the first century, there are those who hold true to the absence of gifts. The Reformers and many church leaders today believe that the gifts of the Spirit are endless and are operative even after the apostolic age.

---

[40] Glen Hinson, *The Significance of Glossolalia in the History of Christianity*.

[41] Ibid.

Johnston writes, "miracles did seem to happen after apostolic times but it was usually hearsay or on historic Christianity's outer fringe. It is interesting to note that as miraculous gifts started making a comeback they seemed to happen within groups whose theology was on a downward spiral." This, in fact caused more of a disbelief rather than what was supposed to enhance the belief of the presence of gifts. Johnston also writes, "During this time of miraculous confusion church at large perceived that the Spirit can get out of hand and they tend to stress tradition and to build up the authority of the church office."[42]

      In addition to its defense, believers are promised that specific signs shall follow them, simply because they believe; they shall cast out devils, lay hands on the sick with healing as a result and will speak with new tongues (Mk 16:17-18). If this is a promise to those who believe, that would include the believers of today which would mandate that the gifts are still in full effect. How can anyone with reasonable thought refute that the gifts no longer exist when so many signs and wonders are occurring on a regular basis? They cannot. As the Scripture does not bear witness of the revocation of such. Many have their own personal definitions of the gifts and how they should be organized; however this section will be addressed through personal experience and Scripture interpretation. We will now review the aforementioned classifications of gifts for simplification.

---

[42]Ibid.

Manifestation Gifts

The manifestation gifts are a category of nine gifts that are available to all through the Holy Spirit. It is important to understand what each gift does and who they benefit. They are designed to edify the body of Christ to impact ministry for the Kingdom of God. These gifts can be given to anyone that the Holy Spirit decides. It provides the insight through the eyes of the One who sees and knows all.[43]

In 1 Corinthians 12:8-11, Paul writes,

> To one there is given through the Spirit a message of wisdom, to another a message of knowledge by means of the same Spirit, to another faith by the same Spirit, to another gifts of healing by that one Spirit, to another miraculous powers, to another prophecy, to another distinguishing between spirits, to another speaking in different kinds of tongues, and to still another the interpretation of tongues. All these are the work of one and the same Spirit, and he distributes them to each one, just as he determines.[44]

The gifts listed above are explained as follows.

The wisdom gift, *sophia*, (σοπηια), wisdom in spiritual things. It is the ability to have spiritual directional insight and application for natural matters.[45] A

---

[43]Ibid.

[44]1 Cor 12:8-11.

[45]W. E. Vine, Merrill F. Unger, William White, Jr., *Vines Complete Expository Dictionary*, 1996, 678.

person operating in this gift will be able to understand how to supernaturally solve problems and offer instructions without prior understanding. It benefits individuals or a group of people with the usage of this gift. This does not equate to any previous biblical or secular education but a divine inspiration for present or future events. This inspiration comes from the heart of God through a vision, thought or dreams which may provide application to a situation. In Acts 6:8-10, Stephen was accused of speaking blasphemous words by false witnesses who agitated the elders and scribes. They were not able to handle the wisdom he displayed when he spoke to them. Of course, it led to entrapment through false accusations and unfortunately Stephen's demise – all because of the wisdom gift.

The knowledge gift, *gnosis* (γνοσισ), subjectively of God's knowledge. It is an accurate spiritual knowing of present, past or future, events in the natural.[46] It benefits individuals or a group of people for a specific time and purpose. It is not the same as the wisdom gift. This does not equate to any information learned, studied, or any previously known human knowledge but a divine inspiration that comes from the heart of God through a vision, thought or physical impression. In Acts 5:1-11 Ananias and Sapphira (husband and wife), sold a piece of their property and agreed that they would hold back part of the money for themselves and only give a part of the money to the church. Of course, nothing was wrong with that; however, they sold the property for one amount but agreed to lie that it was sold for another amount which they would lay at the feet of the apostle. Unfortunately for the couple, Peter received a word of knowledge from the Holy

---

[46]Ibid., 348.

Spirit concerning their deception. When Ananias commenced to defraud the church, Peter asked why he would conspire in his heart to misguide the church when the property belongs to him to do as he will with it. Because the deception of Ananias was unto the Holy Spirit, he dropped dead on the spot. A few hours later, his wife Sapphira confirmed that she was in agreement with her husband, not knowing what had already happened to him. She too experienced the same demise as her husband . . . death. Even though they both conspired in secret, Peter received a word of knowledge from God concerning their secret meeting and judged them accordingly.

The faith gift, *pistis* (πιστισ), primarily, firm persuasion, a conviction based upon hearing (akin to *peitho,* to persuade), is used in the New Testament always of faith in God or Christ, or things spiritual. This gift is required to activate the other gifts; it is faith against all odds - a supernatural alignment to believe in the impossible. It is not the same as saving faith (Eph 2:8-9), but a gift of faith which is for the edification of others. This gift gives opportunity to support those who are of weak faith. In Matthew 14:29, Peter shows extraordinary faith as he steps out of the boat onto the water at the word of Jesus. However the actual walking on water falls under the distinction of the miraculous powers gift.[47]

The healing gift, *iama* (ιαμα), formerly signified a means of healing; "in the New Testament, a healing (the result of the act), used in the plural, healings of divinely imparted gifts in the churches in apostolic times." In Acts 28:8-9, Paul prayed and laid hands on the father of Publius as a result of a blood issue and

---

[47]Ibid., 222.

fever and he was miraculously healed as well as others who were nearby and believed. Peter and John initiated healing through a lame man who sat by the gate called "Beautiful," (Acts 3), which included a creative miracle. Each miraculous healing glorified the power of God through His followers.[48]

The miraculous powers gift, *dunamis,* (δυναμισ), power, inherent ability is used of works of a supernatural origin and character, such as could not be produced or explained by natural agents and means. It is translated as miracles that speed up the natural process without delay - situations that interrupt the normal process of events, as exhibited on the Sea of Galilee when Jesus calmed the storm, (Mt 8:23-27). The ministry of Jesus Christ was inundated with miraculous happenings, signs and wonders on a regular basis. His norm was healing the sick, raising the dead and feeding thousands of people with minimum resources. These miracles were a sign to the people that God was with Jesus and approved of His methods in ministry and can also manifest in His children today.[49]

The prophecy gift, *propheteia,* (προπητεια), signifies the speaking forth of the mind and counsel of God which is the same gift that is mentioned in Romans 12:8. On many occasions, prophecy shares information concerning future events or situations that the individual would not ordinarily know. This does not have the same meaning as "preaching or proclaiming the good news;" although

---

[48]Ibid., 295.

[49]Ibid., 412.

both are vocal expressions, they have separate distinctions and are not used in lieu of one another.[50]

Paul instructs the Church at Corinth to follow after love and for them to desire spiritual gifts especially prophecy (1 Cor 14:1, 3, 4) because prophecy enlightens the church; prophesying is to bring edification, exhortation and comfort to men. As Philip the evangelist extended hospitality to Paul and his band of comrades, his four daughters, began to operate in the gift of prophecy (Acts 21:8). Because one prophesies does not mean that they are considered a prophet (Eph 4:11) but a prophet will always have the ability to prophesy because it is a part of their office.

In earlier times, a group called the Montanists approved the use of "prophecy and spiritual gifts" but not everyone agreed with the movement. In his book, *Church History,* Everett Ferguson discusses the origin of Montanism which was named after its founder, Montanus during the 150s or 170s. He claimed himself to be the Paraclete (Holy Spirit) as spoken of in 1 John 2:1. He along with two women supporters, Priscilla and Maximilla were responsible for the spread of the prophetic movement, called "New Prophecy," by devoted followers, which started in Phrygia but later moved to Asia Minor, Rome and North Africa. There were those who opposed the movement and declared that it was "Phrygian or Kataphrygian heresy." It was believed that those who participated were somehow possessed by a spirit because they spoke in a frantic manner. Their critics objected to this behavior as the biblical prophets were never uncontrollable but they kept

---

[50]Ibid., 492.

possession of their mental faculties. The Montanists worshipped the idea of prophecy and spiritual gifts as the hallmark of apostolic Christianity.[51]

This emphasized differences between the "Montanists and the mainstream church." Ferguson writes, "The dispute over prophecy involved the question of authority in the church: Who has it and how it should be exercised. The Montanists seem not to have opposed the organization of the church, but only to have claimed a place for spiritual gifts as well, but the church's response put the controversy in terms of organization and ministry. The appeal to the authority of the Holy Spirit was countered; it seems, in the church by three developments."

> 1. The first recorded synods of bishops were held in Asia Minor to consider the proper course of action in relation to the Montanists. Such meetings were comparable to a civil council *(koinon)* that brought leaders of the imperial cult in the cities of a province together to discuss matters of common concern. These early meetings of bishops to discuss the working of the Holy Spirit laid the basis in the actual practice of the church for the theory that the Holy Spirit works through a council.
>
> 2. The source of authority in Scripture was emphasized. Montanist prophecy was not true prophecy by biblical standards, it was argued, because it was ecstatic.
>
> 3. The bishops claimed to be the true spiritual leaders of the church, possessing the Holy Spirit by reason of

---

[51]Everett Ferguson, *Church History, From Christ to Pre-Reformation, Volume One,* (Grand Rapids, MI, Zondervan, 2005), 101.

> their office. As the bishops claimed apostolic and teaching authority in the church over against Gnostic teachers, so the bishops countered the Montanist appeal to prophets with their own possession of the Spirit. Thus the early triad of apostles, prophets, and teachers began to be centered now in the bishop.[52]

Even though opposition was great, the following of the Montanist grew as a result of the discontentment that many people had with the Gnostics and their "elitism" idea that they knew more about the move of the spiritual gifts than any other group; they found a group of which they could be a part. In modern day, there are many denominations that feel that they are the only ones who have a clear understanding on the spiritual gifts, the Holy Spirit, or dancing in the Spirit, which can turn into cultic worship rather than a true manifestation of the Holy Spirit. Consequently, there is no one denomination that has all of the knowledge of the Holy Spirit.

The distinguishing between spirits, *discerning*, (διακρισισ), a clear discrimination, is translated discerning of spirits, judging by evidence whether they are evil or of God which spirit is in operation. It is not "fault finding," reading the minds of neither people nor does it give the right to be judgmental about every individual, (Mt 7:1) but the Holy Spirit endows awareness in the spirit realm to identify motivations.[53]

---

[52]Ibid., 102-103.

[53] Vines, 171.

The speaking in different tongues and the interpretation of tongues gift, *glossa* (γλοσσα), the use of the gift of tongues is mentioned as exercised in the gatherings of local churches, speaks of the gift in general terms, and couples with it that of the interpretation of tongues. The gift of tongues is a language that the believer may not understand but God understands the utterance. It is personal communication that is filtered by the Holy Spirit to the Father on the behalf of the believer. The apostle Paul addressed the Church at Corinth concerning the abuse of the gift of tongues, and how it should be used separately and in conjunction with the interpretation of tongues gift in public settings as tongues are for the unbeliever (1 Cor 14).[54]

Jesus gave authority to His twelve disciples (Lk 9:1-2, 6) and the seventy-two disciples to work miracles, signs and wonders (Lk 10:9). These signs continued after the ascension of Jesus, as God "bestowed this sign of authority on the apostles (Acts 15:12) and they transmitted in turn, as part of their own miracle working and the crowning sign of their divine commission, to others, in the form of what the New Testament calls spiritual gifts."[55]

Ministry (Administration) Gifts

The spiritual abilities above give segue to what we identify as the five-fold ministry gifts. The offices, which are considered as the ministry (administration) gifts, are apostles, prophets, evangelists, pastors and teachers, which are listed in

---

[54]Ibid., 636.

[55]Miraculous Gifts in the Early Church http://www.academia.edu/458797/ Miraculous_Gifts
_in_the_Early_Church_A_Historical_Analysis, 3.

Ephesians 4:11, but the local churches do not normally list them as officers. These gifts are how the Holy Spirit administrates in the body of Christ.

The ministry gifts are a category of five, which are people who have been called to the ministry for the sole purpose of equipping and perfecting the saints. It is important to know that one cannot tithe, work hard enough or fast in order to receive a ministry gift. This means that no one can buy a ministry gift because they are rich neither earn a ministry gift because they are faithful and hard working. Just because a parent may have a five-fold ministry call does not automatically bestow that gift upon the child. It is a specific calling from God on specific individuals through the Holy Spirit to enhance the Kingdom of God through equipping the saints for service.[56] In Ephesians 4:11, Paul tells us, that Christ Himself gave the apostles, the prophets, the evangelists, the pastors and teachers, to equip his people for works of service, so that the body of Christ may be built up. If you are called to the five-fold ministry, you are called in at least one of the offices but could stand in more than one as God sees fit.

The apostle, *apostolos* (αποστολοσ), is one sent forth (*apo,* from, *stello,* to send). It is known that the twelve apostles were given a unique place in church history as they were the only ones sent forth with "apostolic authority" and there were no others and will not be any others in this regard. They were the only disciples who could lay claim to their presence at the beginning of Jesus' ministry until His ascension. Therefore, this type of apostleship is restricted to only the twelve, including Judas Iscariot-the betrayer, (Mt 10:4-20) and would not include

---

[56]Fortune, *Discover Your God-Given Gifts*... 16.

Paul in this case. However, Matthias (the replacement of Judas) was numbered with the eleven because he fit the aforementioned criteria for apostleship (Acts 1:21-26). It is also written that Joseph, who was called Barsabas, who was surnamed Justus, was also a candidate for this appointment. Yet there remains a question of who were the other seventy-two that Jesus "sent forth" in Luke 10:1, which included women – were they disciples or apostles? As the chapter continued, Jesus gave them the same specific instructions as He did to His twelve disciples but without any regional restrictions. It is noted in Luke 10:1-12, that Jesus appointed and sent out the seventy-two others two by two unto "every town" where He himself would go but in Matthew 10:1-15, Jesus appointed the twelve and sent them out with restrictions; they could only go to the lost sheep of the house of Israel but were forbidden to go anywhere among the Gentiles or towns of the Samaritans. The latter instructions demanded that the original twelve were bound to serve the lost sheep of the house of Israel for their immediate assignment and the others were to minister to whomever that needed their assistance. When the seventy-two returned, they reported success. A few of the seventy-two were later co-laborers with the apostle Paul, named among the apostles and also selected to care for the Grecian widows in Acts 6:5-6.[57]

    It is an obvious assumption that a higher level of authority was given to the apostles in the early church, due to their life with Jesus, their mission, and their ministry calling (Mk 3:13ff; Acts 1: 21ff.). It has been said that the apostles were the "authentic founders and guides of the early churches." Because they

---

[57] Wernerbiblecommentary.org/?q=book/print/391.

were the ones who walked with Christ throughout His ministry, witnessed the resurrection (visitation) and were commissioned by Him (Acts 1:2-8) alludes to the fact that there could not be any others who could stake this claim to apostleship.[58] Consequently, the belief of many writings shares this sentiment.

However, the New Testament refers to Andronicus and Junia, (who was a woman, possibly the sister or wife of Andronicus), in Romans 16:7 as apostles because they were noted *(episemos-bearing a mark; illustrious)* among the apostles and also "sent forth," and shared in the sufferings of prison.[59] In Thessalonians 1:1, Silvanius and Timotheus worked alongside Paul. There were other brethren mentioned in 2 Corinthians 8:23, as apostles of the churches, James, who was the Lord's brother in Galatians 1:19, Apollos in 1 Corinthians 4:6-9, and Epaphroditus mentioned as your messenger translated as *'your apostle'* in Philippians 2:25. Also the apostle Paul who saw Jesus, as a light on the road to Damascus; one that is sent forth to establish and lay the foundation for the church.[60]

Many times the office of apostle is misconstrued because of the lack of understanding for the appointment. Since the above-mentioned requirements (including a visitation from God) have been established to determine the office of apostles, it is considered that today's apostles are utilizing apostolic authority.

---

[58]W. T. Conner, *Christian Doctrine* (Nashville, TN: Broadman Press, 1937), 263.

[59]Carm.org/junia-apostle.

[60]Vines, 30.

In his book, *On Church Leadership,* Mark Driscoll writes, "In addition to the twelve, Romans, 1 Corinthians, 2 Corinthians, Galatians, Ephesians, Colossians, 1 Timothy, 2 Timothy, and Titus all open with Paul introducing himself as an apostle chosen by Jesus, . . ." even though he did not serve with the actual twelve. Driscoll writes, "A reading of Acts also shows how Paul ministered cross-culturally and planted churches. (Gal 2:8; 1 Pt 1:1). Although we do not have apostles in the vein of Paul and Peter today, the function of their office does continue in a limited sense . . ." as Paul was limited to only reach the Gentiles. The other individuals named as apostles outside of the twelve, (in addition to Paul), were gifted persons who effectively ministered cross-culturally, organized, established and planted churches in various locations. It is to this end that Christian leaders and individuals who follow in this manner operate in the gift of the apostle.[61]

In his writings, *The Ministry Gifts,* Kenneth Hagin list an explanation of four classes of apostles this way:

1. Jesus the Chief Apostle (Heb 3:1) – Jesus is the only One that can hold this class of apostleship. He is the Apostle and High Priest of our profession who was sent from God to make atonement for the sins of the world.

2. Apostles of the Lamb (Acts 1:16-22) – the original twelve were eyewitnesses of the life of Jesus, His death, burial and resurrection. They were the first to be able to give testimony of what they have seen and experienced.

---

[61]Driscoll, 11.

3. New Testament Apostles (Acts 14:14) – This would include Paul, Barnabas and the other apostles who assisted with laying the foundation for establishing churches which was an entirely different mission than the original twelve apostles.

4. Apostles of Today (Eph 4:11) – This group of apostles is designed to equip and teach the saints to operate in biblical order until we all come into the unity of the faith.[62]

Driscoll writes, "Ultimately, the apostle Paul and the twelve apostles in the early church and those gifted with the role of apostle in the present day are not spiritual authorities unto themselves, but rather under the leadership of Jesus, whom the Scripture, Hebrews 3:1 calls the Apostle. This suggests that anyone who proclaims apostleship outside of the confines of Scripture is doomed and considered a false apostle (2 Cor 11:13; Rev 2:2) and delusional super-apostles (2 Cor 11:5; 12:11)." This is unfortunately true for those who are disobedient to true authority but considers themselves to be the final authority overriding Scripture; for example, cult leaders and those who present the Scriptures in error.[63]

The prophet, *prophetes* (προπητεσ), one who speaks forth unrehearsed inspirational revelation of future events that always comes to past as guided by the Holy Spirit; a proclaimer of a divine message as God reveals, without fear of

---

[62] Kenneth Hagin, *The Ministry Gifts, Fourth Edition,* (Rhema Bible Training Center, Broken Arrow, OK, 1992), 24.

[63] Ibid.

repercussions.[64] One who speaks the heart of God and changes peoples' lives. This gift is confirmed by prophecy, word of wisdom and knowledge, discerning of spirits and healings to bear witness of the call as a prophet (1 Kgs 17:1-24). This ministry gift is another gift that was given a unique place in church history. In the New Testament, the word prophet is used in the churches to identify the office. More often used as a person activated in the office of the prophet versus prophecy as listed in 1 Corinthians 12:10 and Romans 12:6. It is assumed that there was no specific rank or order for the prophetic, but the gift of the prophetic was bestowed on particular individuals in the church only when it was needed. Driscoll asserts that, "Prophets were probably functionaries rather than officials; that is, prophecy was speaking forth a message under the direct inspiration of the Spirit." It was considered a short-term manifestation that could be imparted to anyone in the church in order to accomplish the immediate task.[65]

    In the Old Testament, there were many male prophets, *nabi* who proclaimed under divine inspirational words from God. Some of the more popular named prophets were Elijah, Elisha, Samuel, Ezekiel, Jeremiah, Isaiah, and Jonah. Some of the prophets had men to follow and learn from them which the usage of *nabi* in that instance would mean companion or follower of a prophet. The distinction of *nabi* is also meant for false prophets. There were also a few woman prophets *(nbiah)* of the Old Testament who were also used as mouthpieces for God. Their names were Deborah, Miriam, Huldah, and Isaiah's wife, which usage

---

[64]Ibid., 27.

[65]Driscoll, 13.

of *nbiah* may mean a companion or follower of a prophet and Noadiah, who was deemed as a false prophet.[66]

Often, the office of the prophet is misused which causes people to fear their presence and what they might say. In the Old Testament, God sent prophets to announce soon coming events and even to pronounce judgment. In the New Testament, Agabus was named a prophet who gave news of an impending famine that would take place throughout the world (Acts 11:27-29). This same prophet foretold the persecution that Paul would endure during his visit to Jerusalem (Acts 21:10-11). Although none of the Early Church Fathers have disavowed this prophecy, some scholars have refuted the words of Agabus, because it was not carried out word for word. Despite this minuscule assumption, the circumstances in which Paul was accosted and detained by the Jews and Romans were detailed enough as Agabus quoted the Holy Spirit as the Provider of the aforementioned prophecy.[67] Although in the New Testament there was an instance referring to women who prophesied (Acts 21:9), only one is listed as a prophetess *(prophetis),* which is the feminine of prophet; her name was Anna (Lk 2:36-37). She was eighty-four years old, widowed, and lived in the temple.

The evangelist, *euangelistes* (ευαγγελιστησ), is a messenger of good news which denotes a preacher of the gospel, which makes clear the distinctiveness of the functions in the churches and is a fruitful soul winner. This person effectively draws people to Christ and leads them to salvation. This gift is

---

[66]Vines, 493.

[67]Nathan Busenitz, *Throwing Prophecy under the* Agabus, (The Cripplegate, March 15, 2012).

confirmed by miracles, signs and wonders, in order to bear witness of the word that is preached (Acts 8:5-7).[68] Paul instructed Timothy to do the work of an evangelist, (2 Tim 4:5), as a pastor and teacher. However, Philip was the only person mentioned in the New Testament who bore the gift of an evangelist, (Acts 21:8).When Philip left for Samaria, he preached the gospel to the people, they believed and were baptized afterward the apostles were sent in order to lay hands on the people that they may receive the Holy Spirit (Acts 8:12-17). As an evangelist, Philip completed his phase of ministry in Samaria by preaching the gospel, baptizing and manifesting miracles and signs as a witness. Therefore, the apostles fulfilled their responsibility after the work of the evangelist was done.[69]

In churches today, the term evangelist is often misappropriated in many denominations. Some will give first time preachers this distinction as the "first step" into the ministry as if the office of the evangelist is something that goes away when another gift is discovered. If one is called as another gift in the five-fold ministry, they will still be an evangelist in addition to the other gift(s) that God gave them as it will activate when it is necessary. Often, women ministers who are given the opportunity to preach are frequently labeled by the term "evangelist" as a way to seemingly minimize their authority in the ministry or lessen their equality with their male minister counterparts. Both situations are an incorrect display of this gift as gifts are genderless and forever.

---

[68]Vines, 208.

[69]Hagin, 42.

The pastor, *poimen* (ποιμεν), a shepherd, one who tends herds or flocks (not merely one who feeds them), is used metaphorically of Christian pastors, who guide as well as feed the flock and have a heart for the people. One that nurtures, cares for, and oversees the people after they have been led into salvation; however, they are also teachers of the word. There were a few pastors assigned to local churches in the New Testament, but Timothy and Titus were the most familiar pastors mentioned. Although the office of pastor is not listed in further Scriptures, it is implied as Paul assigned them to visit churches in Ephesus (1 Tim 1:3) and Crete (Ti 1:5) to give the saints guidance; they were responsible for teaching, instructing, appointing and rebuking, which were pastoral duties.[70]

Those who have been called to the office of pastor will often activate in the manifestations of the word of wisdom, knowledge, tongues and interpretation as gifts operating in their ministry. These gifts will allow the pastor to clearly understand the needs of the people as God reveals the hearts of men to the pastor. A person called into this ministry gift has the tasks of an under shepherd, as overseeing the flock will require their consistent undivided attention.[71] There is a further detailed description on the role of pastor and its components in Chapter 3, Leadership Roles in the Church.

The teacher, *didaskalous* (διδασκαλουσ), which is rendered as a teacher or teachers of the truth in the churches which is used in conjunction with the

---

[70]Vines, 462.

[71]Hagin, 52.

above-mentioned ministry gifts, pastor. They are all apt to expound on the word of God with an effective outcome through a supernatural ability.[72] Teaching was considered an essential task in the New Testament. It was most likely a role that was taken on by prophets (Acts 13:1) and pastors and others, even though it was probably a main duty of the pastor to teach. Barnabas and Paul were prophets/teachers and later fulfilled their call as apostles (Acts 14:14). Paul lists pastor and teacher together as if they are the same office with two separate purposes (Eph 4:11). Some have even called this section of gifts the four-fold ministry versus the five-fold ministry because of this distinction. However, each of the ministry gifts has the mandate to be teachers of the word.[73]

Consequently, Geoffrey Guns discuss two concerns involving teachers and the effectiveness of ministry, in churches of today. He writes,

> First, we must be concerned about what is taught. Does what we teach enrich and increase spiritual growth and ministry effectiveness? What is taught in church or in training sessions must make a real difference in the lives of people and in the life of the church. When spiritual gifts are taught then current and potential leaders will be able to identify where they fit in the larger scheme of things. Second, we must be concerned about who is teaching. What is the level of knowledge, personal character and public reputation of the teacher? The ministry of teaching is a spiritual gift given to the church for the purpose of building up the church for the work of ministry (Ro 12:7; 1 Cor 12:28-29; Eph 4:11; 1 Jn 3:1). Leaders are held to a

---

[72]Ibid., 619.

[73]Conner, 263-264.

> higher standard of excellence as they are called to equip the church through their gift of teaching.[74]

In order to equip the saints for ministry, God set biblical order in place to accomplish this purpose through the person of Jesus Christ. The Holy Spirit is the agent in whom this structure of leadership employs simply ". . . to create a people whose life is a witness to Jesus Christ." Darrell L. Guder writes, "This point is most vivid in Paul's description of the constitution of the church in Ephesians 4. His directions for leadership emerge from his understanding of the life and ministry of Jesus Christ. This biblical perspective illustrates that the formation of a redeemed community of the Kingdom is essential to the focus of missional leadership."[75]

In the churches of today, many leaders of ministries fall prey to desires of the flesh or leave the ministry due to overwhelming demands that are placed on them by the congregation to live their lives above reproach. Once they fall, then they are tagged by the phrase, "I thought they were a preacher or a man/woman of the cloth and they were so gifted." Truthfully, they are still a preacher or a man/woman of the cloth and gifted because of the call that God has on them; the call does not change because of indiscretions. Paul tells the Christians at Ephesus that Jesus left gifts for the church in the form of people that were apostles, prophets, evangelists, pastors and teachers, "in order that the church fulfills its present task (Eph 4:12), and, at the end, reach the goal set for her (Eph 4:13)."

---

[74]Guns, *Spiritual Leadership: A Guide* . . . 21.

[75]Guder, 184-185.

The former alignment will equip the body of Christ through the Holy Spirit for service in order to empower the masses.[76]

It is indicated in Ephesians 4, how the "Spirit calls leaders for the church." Everyone is not called as an evangelist, even though some may be able to rightly divide the word of truth and effectively draw people to Christ, but all can minister the good news. The gifts are given as the Spirit sees fit. "No matter what specific forms leadership may take at any point in time, the Spirit guides leadership in order to bring into reality a future—present messianic community of the reign of God, and the Spirit equips that leadership to lead the community into missional engagement with the context in which they live." Each person leads according to their God-given gifts.[77]

Although there are many scholars and philosophers who adamantly discredit the existence and use of these gifts today, it is with great conviction and biblical support that the Holy Spirit still has the ability to use whomever He chooses in order to equip, exhort and edify the body of Christ for the work of the Kingdom of God. It is to this end to know that as long as the Church exists, gifts will be needed until we all come into the unity of the faith, (Eph 4:11-13).

Motivational (Operation) Gifts

The motivational gifts are a category of seven gifts that are a part of the personality of an individual which they receive at their creation. They are not

---

[76]Ibid.

[77]Ibid., 187.

earned but given to us for the benefit of others. These are divine endowments that God allocates for specific service through people with these precise motivations.[78]

In Romans 12:6-8, Paul writes,

> We have different gifts, according to the grace given to each of us. If your gift is prophesying, then prophesy in accordance with your faith; if it is serving, then serve; if it is teaching, then teach; if it is to encourage, then give encouragement; if it is giving, then give generously; if it is to lead, do it diligently; if it is to show mercy, do it cheerfully.[79]

The prophecy gift, *propheteia,* (προπηετεια), signifies the speaking forth of the mind and counsel of God, that which is prophesied and synonymous with the prophecy gift that is found in 1 Corinthians 12:10. Because one can prophesy (1 Cor 12:10, Ro 12:6) does not insinuate that they are a prophet as listed in Ephesians 4:11, but a prophet will always be able to prophesy because prophecy is a part of the office of the prophet. In Acts 11:28, there was a man named Agabus who prophesied that there would be a famine in all of the inhabited places in the world. Scriptures also confirmed that the prophecy came to past. Some of the areas that a person with this type of gift would function best are as an intercessory prayer leader, assisting a pastor or fasting with definite results.[80]

---

[78]Fortune, *Discover Your God-Given Gifts...*17.

[79]Ro 12:6-8.

[80]Vines, 492.

The serving gift, *diakonia,* (διακονια), is rendered as service or serving. This is a gift that gives the server great pleasure in looking for ways in which to serve others and assisting with their personal or ministry endeavors; they provide great assistance to those who are called in the five-fold ministry by providing support in any way that God directs. Many times they meet the practical needs of others with finesse and humility. In Luke 10:40, it is written that Martha, who was also sitting at the feet of Jesus became distracted with much serving, so much that she wanted her sister Mary to get up and assist her with the work. This gift is often called the "ministry of helps" which could include talents such as singing, artistry or other talents that support the ministry of the body of Christ. Some of the areas that a person with this type of gift would function best are as a babysitter, housekeeper, waiter/waitress, pastor's care assistance, kitchen service or handyman.[81]

The teaching gift, *didaskalia* (διδασκαλια), translated as doctrine, that which is taught, teaching and instruction; the ability to teach difficult material through practical methods to help students clearly understand. This is not the same translation that is used in the teacher *(didaskalous)* which is written in Ephesians 4:11. In Titus 2:1, Paul instructed Titus to teach sound doctrine to the inhabitants on the Island of Crete and instruct them, with all authority, in the way to live. Some of the areas that a person with this type of gift would function best are a Church school, Bible study teacher, tutor, or researcher.[82]

---

[81]Ibid., 563.

[82]Ibid., 180.

The encouraging gift, *paraklesis* (παρακλεσισ), encouraging appropriately to exhort; primarily, to call to a person, "to one's aid," denotes to call on, entreat, to admonish, to urge one to pursue some course of conduct; they are apt to stir up the hearts of people through encouragement. Often referred to as an exhorter. Someone who communicates believable words of hope to bring comfort to an otherwise dismal situation. Some of the areas that a person with this type of gift would function best are a crisis center/prayer counselor, call center representative, or on an outreach team.[83]

The giving gift, *metadidomi* (μεταδιδομι), to give a share of, impart and that generously. Often referred to as a giver. Someone who finds joy in giving not only money but any resource that can be shared in a liberal manner to meet the needs of others; they always seem to have the resources to provide. The giver may contribute things that they actually need themselves but will share it nonetheless. Sometimes abusers may try to manipulate and take advantage of the giver knowing that they are free-hearted and generous in sharing their reserves. In order to ensure accurate distribution, the giver should pray for guidance to appropriately allocate resources for ministry. Some of the areas that a person with this type of gift would function best is a crusader, fundraiser, outreach volunteer, or in street witnessing.[84]

---

[83] Ibid., 217.

[84] Ibid., 265.

The leading gift, *diakonia* (διακονια), is the office and work of a *diakonos* of apostolic ministry of the service of believers, ministration. Because one is able to lead and effectively organize, does not automatically qualify them as an apostle or pastor (Eph 4:11), without having a calling from God.[85] A person with this gift is someone that organizes, directs events and keeps people focused and orderly. In her book, *Reach Me with SMILES,* Barbara A. F. Brehon writes, "The question is not only whether or not we have teachers teaching who are not gifted to teach, but do we have leaders leading who have neither the gift of administration, nor the understanding of the necessity for a gift-based ministry." This deficiency can lead to the uselessness of leadership.[86]

Consequently, there are many frustrations that are prevalent when trying to find individuals with appropriate leadership gifts. Some may boast on their leadership skills by way of spoken credentials but when put to task, the unproductive manifestation of their said abilities comes to naught. It is then realized that they either lack relational skills, have difficulty-motivating people, have the wrong attitude or they simply do not possess the administrative skill set that it takes to maintain order. It is at this point that they recognize that their deception has been uncovered and then they just quit in midstream from conviction and pressure of the task. Nevertheless, a development process is

---

[85]Ibid., 411.

[86]Barbara A. F. Brehon, *Reach Me with SMILES.* (Lithonia, GA: Orman Press, Inc., 2005), 85.

needed to produce what is already available to them. A leader should identify what type of leadership style informs their direction.

There are a few styles of leadership that would be appropriate to list. According to an article written on *Leadership Styles,* asserts that "Leadership style is the manner and approach of providing direction, implementing plans, and motivating people."[87] The following three are listed.

> Authoritarian (Autocratic) - this style has been a traditional approach in times past. Only one person has all the power and possesses the decision making abilities. There is no consultation with the employee nor is input allowed. Rather, the employee is to follow instructions without any explanation. The atmosphere for motivation is based on punishments and rewards. Unfortunately, this type of leadership renders a larger resistance in an organization.[88]

When is the Authoritarian leadership style effective? When there are new trainees who do not know how to perform the task, when detailed instructions are necessary, when employees do not respond to any other leadership style, when the manager's authority is challenged, when there has been poor management within a specific department, when other departments are involved, when there is little time for a decision to be made.[89]

---

[87] nwlink.com/~donclark/leader/leadstl.html.

[88] vectorstudy.com/management_topics/autocratic_leadership.htm.

[89] Ibid.

It is also worthy to note the other side to this leadership style. When is the Authoritarian leadership style not effective? When there is severe absenteeism, low morale, employees have fear and resentment, when employees are not dependent upon their manager, or when employees want their opinion heard.[90]

This style of leadership was the model in the churches of old. Typically, the pastor or deacon was the only voice to follow and the parishioners obeyed with little to any challenge. Today, fewer churches operate under this type of leadership. It can be both productive and non-productive but can be used when the correct situation presents itself to be appropriate.

> Democratic (Participative Leadership) - this style incorporates and solicits the opinion and ideas of employees. The manager keeps everyone in the loop on decisions and resolutions. This leadership style renders the manager more as a coach with the final say rather than the one making all of the decision without aid.[91]

When is the Democratic leadership style effective? When a manager wants to encourage team building, when the manager involves employees in matters that will affect them, when a manager wants to encourage achievement and personal growth in their employees.[92]

When is the Democratic leadership style not effective? When there is little to any time to get employee input, when mistakes cannot be made, when safety of

---

[90]Ibid.

[91]Ibid.

[92]nwlink.com/~donclark/leader/leadstl.html.

employees is a concern, when it is more cost effective for the manager to make the final decision.[93]

This style of leadership has taken over by leaps and bounds in modern day churches. Over the last few years people have been taught that their opinion matters and that they have a right to give input to the final outcome. Many of these people are professionals and often times hold secular executive and management positions and will not receive dictatorship as is with the Authoritarian leadership style. If the Democratic style is used, it brings management and employees together to accomplish one goal. It allows more creativity and participation from everyone who has any knowledge that will be helpful.

> Laissez-Faire (Delegate) - this style is in many ways "self-directed." The employee is left to his or her own resources, decisions and resolutions. There is little to no input from the manager. The word Laissez-Faire is the noninterference in the affairs of others. [French : laissez, second person pl. imperative of laisser, to let, allow + faire, to do].[94]

When is the Laissez-Faire leadership style effective? When employees are experts in their field, when employees need minimal supervision, when "outside experts" are used, and employees are trustworthy to follow protocol.[95]

---

[93] Ibid.

[94] vectorstudy.com/management_topics/autocratic_leadership.htm.

[95] nwlink.com/~donclark/leader/leadstl.htm.

When is the Laissez-Faire leadership style not effective? When managers cannot praise employees for their good work, when managers cannot provide regular feedback to employees, when employees do not understand their role or responsibilities, when employees are insecure about the unavailability of management, this style will not be the best to use.[96]

This style of leadership is a godsend to those who are leaders themselves as it allows them to be creative and exercise their gifts without receiving harassing input by their superior who may not have the wherewithal to think outside of the box. On the other hand, it is a nightmare for those who are less creative and unmotivated. They tend to desire the attention of the leader and demand their step-by-step directions to avoid making their own mistakes. Some churches have leaders who operate in this manner which can destroy a ministry if the congregants are not experts in their field of service. In contrast, it can afford the opportunity to those who are experts to excel but may give them too much leverage which can cause a challenge with assumed authority over the set leadership.

Either three of these styles of leadership can be productive or nonproductive depending on the task at hand and the structure of an organization. The leadership should exercise wisdom as to which style would be feasible administration for maximum impact.

With the above in mind, some of the areas that a person with the lead or administration gift would function best are an office manager, executive

---

[96] Ibid.

administrator, event planner, coordinator group leader or Christian Education Director.[97]

The mercy gift, *eleeo* (ελεεο), signifies, in general, to feel empathy with the misery of another, and especially empathy manifested in act, to have pity or mercy shown. Often referred to as one who shows compassion. Some of the vocations that a person with this type of gift would function best in are a nursing home attendant, prison ministry leader or feeder of the homeless.[98]

Interestingly, the author has often heard various people denounce the idea that they have been given a gift at all. Some feel that everyone else has a gift but not them. There are those who do not know why they act the way that they do but it all comes down to the way in which they have been programmed.[99] It is calamitous to know that many people will die without fulfilling their destiny or discovering their gift(s), because they will never reach the capacity or make the impact in which God desires for them. The church suffers overall while the mission of discipleship becomes more difficult to accomplish, if the variety of gifts are not used properly or if they are ineffectively misdirected.

As we review the various categories of gifts, we can find them combined but in set order as God intends for them to operate in the church. Let us look at them together.

---

[97] Ibid., 411.

[98] Ibid., 404.

[99] Fortune, *Discover Your God-Given Gifts*... 14.

In Corinthians 12:28, Paul writes:

> And God hath set some in the church, first apostles, secondarily prophets, thirdly teachers, after that miracles, then gifts of healings, helps, governments, diversities of tongues. are all apostles? are all prophets? are all teachers? are all workers of miracles? Have all gifts of healing? Do all speak with tongues? do all interpret? But covet earnestly the best gifts: and yet shew I unto you a more excellent way.[100]

The above Scripture reveals how the church should operate in the body of Christ. The apostles and prophets were the ones set for the foundation of the Church (Eph 2:20) with the New Testament revelation for the body of Christ. The teachers will include those who are evangelists, pastors, bishops, overseers and elders. They are designed to spread the message of the Kingdom of God to the masses. The miracles, gifts of healing, helps, governments and diversities of tongues are all in support of the ministry gifts that precede it for the edifying of the body of Christ. The apostle Paul instructs the Church at Corinth to move beyond the norm to "earnestly desire the higher gifts. And I will show you a still more excellent way (1 Cor 12:31)." Even though the above gifts are exciting to have, a more excellent way is delivered in Chapter 13, through faith, hope and love.

The understanding of each person's gift is necessary to be an empowered leader. Even though each person possesses at least one primary gift and a diversity of gifts in part, the Scriptures suggest that each gift is best exercised

---

[100] 1 Cor 12:28-31.

when used with maturity, unity and love. Since gifts can be given to anyone as the Holy Spirit chooses, one cannot assume because a leader is gifted that they are closer to God or have the "salvation lifestyle" under their control – this would be a gross negligence of thought. However, it is the well-developed character of an individual that determines how much time has been spent with God.

As Paul discusses each category of gifts, he never fails to mention the character traits that should accompany the usage of gifts: Maturity – a successful leader must learn to react and respond in a mature manner when relating to others. It is important to ensure daily growth from various challenges in order to teach others how to overcome their obstacles. A leader should work at a higher level of excellence (Eph 4:14); Unity – a successful leader must learn that even though there may be great diversity within a team, it will be wise to understand that each team member has his or her own uniqueness in the group and each section must work as a cohesive unit as everyone is necessary (1 Cor 12:12-28); Love – a successful leader learns how to talk and walk in love, which is a command from God. All leaders should exemplify this as others follow this example. Love must be sincere with a forgiving heart as it is practiced daily. Put love in action, it will never fail (Ro 12:9-10).

God calls leaders for His purpose which will not be self-serving to the leader. God strategically assigns leaders to various locales to impact the world for the Kingdom. One must understand that it is the will of God to lead the individual toward a purposeful outcome. In *Spiritual Leadership: A Guide to Developing Spiritual Leaders in the Church*, Geoffrey V. Guns writes, "The church is a spiritual organism, called into being by God to achieve the purposes of God in the world. Therefore, those who lead are called by God to fulfill God's purpose and not their own agenda."[101] Christian leaders are handpicked by God. They are chosen with a specific assignment in mind. Guns continue to write, "Christian leadership is accepting the call of God to use spiritual gifts to minister to the masses for the Kingdom of God among and with a specific group of people. This definition makes several points about the distinctiveness of Christian leadership."[102]

Leroy Eims, in his book *Be The Leader You Were Meant To Be: Biblical Principles Of Leadership* suggests, ". . . When someone comes to ask you to serve in one way or another, make certain that God is directing the assignment. Do not budge an inch in either direction until you have determined the will of God in the matter." God has revealed His will to us through His word. Eims further writes that, "Since God is concerned with what we do; God will distinguish His will. God promises to do so. 'I will instruct thee and teach thee in the way which thou shalt go: I will guide thee with Mine eye.'" As God continues to instruct, teach and guide, one cannot help but to know His will for their life.[103]

---

[101] Guns, *Spiritual Leadership: A Guide . . .* , 45.

[102] Ibid., 21.

[103] Eims, 9.

CHAPTER 3

Leadership Roles in the Church

The officers, as outlined in 1 Timothy 3:1-13, provide written protocol for biblical leaders "…through prophecy with the laying on of hands by the council of elders (4:14)." The biblical account found in 1 Timothy 3 and Titus 1 gives a road map toward who may be qualified to lead or rule in the administration of the church. The biblical account is the lead qualification but it is not the qualification that is given priority in our ministry context. Many times, the biblical account is not always the leading selection criteria as to the qualifications of a current or potential leader because of the constitution and polity of a church or even a personal preference. The modern day process in which people are selected for leadership roles is worth dissecting. Corresponding with the New Testament, the Christians were prayerful in their selection consideration as the church leaders and congregants collectively sought the Holy Spirit for direction. Having the opportunity to participate in leadership selection should not be viewed as an opening to promote individuals to leadership positions simply because they have seniority or because they are personally favored over another. This process may not yield the best candidate for the position as their skills may not be adequate.

In many cases, the church selects current or potential leaders based on their secular specialized skills, instead of their personal character and family life. The emphasis in the former, and not the latter, can directly conflict with the biblical description of a qualified leader. However, there are situations in which the church body demands that the current or potential leader has specific credentials which are not considered necessary in the biblical context of leadership. More specifically, a church may require that higher education would be an essential qualification for leadership in order for the potential leader to serve in any capacity. Or, they must be in a particular age group, specific gender, race or their marital status must line up to the qualifications of the church. In any instance, the desires of the membership may be the determining factor in leader selection, which may not be in the best interest of the church.[104] We cannot ignore the fact that numerous churches disregard whom God approves as His leader for their choice of whom they feel the leader should be. This popular preference could allow the selecting of a puppet instead of a pastor.

We understand that the New Testament validates the offices of pastors and deacons in the local church, but we see in modern day church that various officers have been added to the list of officials because of the need to accomplish a variety of tasks. The biblical validation of the two offices does not prevent the selection of additional officials if needed to ensure a functional purpose. Conner writes, "Certain it is that churches since then, even those claiming to follow most closely the New Testament, have had various other officers; such as clerk, treasurer, trustee, Sunday school superintendent, and so forth. On what ground can this be justified? On the ground of necessity." These appointments are primarily made to ensure the task of the church is continued responsibly. Conner writes, "The commission given to us justifies us in using any means or adopting any methods that are consistent with the principles of the gospel and the fundamentals of

---

[104]Benjamin L. Merkle. *Why Elders? A Biblical and Practical Guide for Church Members* (Grand Rapids, MI: Published by Kregel Publications, 2009), 11.

ecclesiology, such as a regenerated church membership and a democratic organization of the church." However, this should not be the standard in the elections of leaders as it is known in contemporary settings, as it would cause the misplacement of leaders who may not be empowered or called to the position.[105]

The administrational composition of a church governs the methods and prerequisites that are crucial for leadership selection. Depending on the structural dynamics of a church, many congregations use the majority vote process to select their leaders and then the senior leader of the church usually decides the formation of the remaining staff. In some cases there is a bishop that presides over the appointment of leaders.[106]

Even though there is a need for officers in the church, it is possible for a church to exist without officers as long as someone performs the functions of an officer. However, if a church has officers who may lack regeneration, the church cannot survive because "it would then cease to possess the Spirit of Christ and would necessarily cease to function as His body." Therefore, the person executing the function of an officer should be born again; being born again is necessary for regeneration. If a Spirit-led person is the assigned leader, the church can function appropriately but if they have not been transformed as a new creature in Christ then the church will not function as His body. There are many churches that have

---

[105]Ibid., 265.

[106]Ibid., 11.

officers in place but they lack the Spirit of Christ to guide their performance; "yet a church cannot do its best work without officers."[107]

All current and potential leaders should realize the need for development in character and skill sets as they will handle the business of souls and the business of the church. There is not any leadership role that should be taken lightly or frivolously mishandled, as all words or deeds should be done as unto the Lord Jesus, giving thanks to God the Father through Him (Col 3:17). There are a few helpful hints that will assist a current or potential leader to begin to understand how to fulfill any church leadership role to which they may be appointed. They are as follows:

Identify the leadership role - each leader must first discover who he or she is and what his or her function is. God has made each person unique and special that no one in the world is exactly like anyone else (Chapter 2). Jesus knows His identity, I am the light of the world (Mt 27:43); I am the Son of God (Jn 9:5); I am the way and the truth and the life (Jn 14:6).

Training for the leadership role – each leader should receive training in his or her field of discovery. This will hone the craft of the leader and will ensure their confidence to carry out the mission of the church. Jesus sent the seventy-two in the training field with instructions, "After this the Lord appointed seventy-two others and sent them two by two ahead of him to every town and places he was about to go . . ." (Lk 10:1-16); they received on the job training.

---

[107]Ibid., 262-263.

Become a mentee in the leadership role – after each leader is trained, they should submit to mentoring while exercising their new skills of leadership. Jesus gives insight to His disciples when it seemed as though they needed more training. They exclaimed, "Why we were not able to put the demon out . . . but this kind does not go out but by prayer and by going without food so you can pray better" (Mt 17:14-21). They had unbelief.

Assess progress in assuming the leadership role - each leader will receive follow-up once identifying, training and mentoring is done. This will bring a refreshing to the leader and also instill necessary information. "All this I have spoken while still with you. But the Advocate, the Holy Spirit, whom the Father will send in my name . . . and will remind you of everything I have said to you" (Jn 14:26).

Often, we desire leaders who are polished but Jesus chose those who had yet to be transformed because He knew their potential. When Peter, and Andrew (casting their nets), James and John (mending their nets) were called to service they were professional fishers (Mt 14:18-22). Jesus utilized their profession to explain their purpose. They entered the period of discipleship when Jesus called them to use their secular profession of fishers but with a different element, as catchers of men. As He gave instructions to people who were professionals at their craft, they agreed to follow his advice even before they knew what He wanted them to do. He met them on the level of their intellect and understanding. In *Activism That Makes Sense: Congregations and Community Organizations,* Gregory E. Augustine Pierce writes, "Many clergy and laity have accepted - intellectually, emotionally, and spiritually - the need for active involvement in the problems of the world in order to fulfill the basic religious mission . . . They just don't know how to do it successfully." However, Jesus was successful as He generated buy-in from those in whom He chose by showing them a fruitful outcome for their profession but for a greater purpose.[108]

In His book, *Becoming a Fruit-Bearing Disciple,* Terry Thomas writes, "Jesus' disciples did not focus primarily on learning His words, but they focused on learning His lifestyle."[109] Jesus is the epitome of what a chosen and consecrated leader should be which should be the desire for each Christian leader who anticipates success. Charles A. Tidwell writes that, ". . . a study of the total approach of Jesus in relation to His apostles shows Him clearly in the roles preparing them to minister. He furnished them the essentials for performing ministry." He equipped them to do greater things than He did while on earth.[110]

Jesus was often moved with compassion as He was among the multitudes of people and His disciples. It was innate behavior for Him as a leader to recognize the need and provide the solution. Jesus identified the need when He saw the crowds of people and likened them to sheep without a shepherd, so He began to impart knowledge of the Kingdom for their benefit.[111] Maxwell writes,

---

[108] Gregory E. Augustine Pierce, *Activism That Makes Sense: Congregations and Community Organizations* (Chicago, IL: ACTA Publications, 1984), 8.

[109] Terry Thomas, *Becoming a Fruit-Bearing Disciple* (Raleigh, NC: Voice of Rehoboth, 2005), 68.

[110] Charles A. Tidwell. *Church Administration: Effective Leadership for Ministry* (Nashville, TN: Boardman Press, 1985), 41.

[111] Mt 9:35-40.

"The leaders of the Bible let their followers know they cared. Jesus was the most caring leader of all time . . . He performed impossible feats, not to impress people with magical ability in order to stretch resources, but rather out of compassion and kindness."[112]

God made the promise that He had pastors that He has already chosen that have His heart concerning the flock (Jer 3:15). According to Adam Clarke's Commentary, the pastor in this passage could mean kings, prophets or both. However, God is the One who has qualified the pastor to feed the people with knowledge of the Divine truth about God which will be a benefit to man, and the things that are pertinent to their salvation. The pastor will also feed the flock with understanding through the preaching of the Gospel of the Kingdom that the people may become "wise, Holy and happy" in His service.[113]

Pastor

The office of pastor has been the most discussed leader in the New Testament but, used interchangeably with other titles such as (1) elder, (2) overseer or bishop, and (3) shepherd. W. T. Conner writes,

> The most significant officer in the New Testament as connected with a local church was that of pastor. There are three terms used in the New Testament for that office- pastor, elder, and bishop. In Acts 20, in the account of Paul's meeting with the elders of the church at Ephesus, in verse 17, they are called elders, while in verse 28 Paul calls

---

[112] Maxwell, 63-64.

[113] Adam Clarke. *Commentary on Jeremiah 3:15. The Adam Clarke Commentary.* http://www.studylight.org/commentaries/acc/view.cgi?bk=jer&ch=3. 1832.

> them bishops (AS). The verb translated feed in verse 28 means to tend as a shepherd, act as shepherd. This is the verb corresponding to the noun that is translated pastor. So here in one passage, the same men are called elders and bishops and they are exhorted to pastor the flock. Again, in Titus 1:5, 7, Paul uses the terms elders and bishops to apply to the same office. In 1 Peter 5:1, 2, Peter addresses the elders, and exhorts them to pastor or shepherd the flock.[114]

In the New Testament, there is not a definitive description of a job description for the pastor to adhere. Conner writes,

> Evidently they were intended to exercise general oversight in spiritual matters, teach their people, and guide in all the activities of the church. Their character and spiritual attainments must be such as to qualify them for such leadership (1 Tm 3: 1ff.; Ti 1: 5ff.; 1 Pt 5: 1ff.).[115] Church government and, thus, church leaders are important because they are given the task of teaching the congregation the word of God. As such, it is crucial that those who teach the word are adequately gifted and trained to accurately handle the word of Truth (2 Tim).[116]

In Acts 14:23; 1 Timothy 5:17 the two terms overseer and elder are used interchangeably. Benjamin L. Merkle writes,

> There are three texts that clearly demonstrate this usage (Acts 20:17, 28; Ti 1:5, 7; 1 Pt 5:1-2). Upon returning from his third missionary journey, Paul's ship harbored at

---

[114]Conner, 264.

[115]Ibid.

[116]Merkle, 12.

Miletus for a few days. Knowing that he might not return to the region again, Paul decided to contact the leaders of the church at Ephesus. Luke informs us that Paul "sent to Ephesus and called the *elders* of the church to come to him" (Acts 20:17, emphasis added). After the elders arrive, Paul gives them a sort of "farewell speech." He exhorts them, "Pay careful attention to yourselves and to all the flock, in which the Holy Spirit has made you *overseers,* to care for the church of God" (20:28, emphasis added). Thus, in verse 17 Paul summons the "elders," but in verse 28 we read that the Holy Spirit made them "overseers." This usage demonstrates that the biblical writer did not make a distinction between the two terms.[117]

Paul elaborates further in Titus 1:5-7 concerning the synonymous terms of elder and overseer. He shares with Titus, "This is why I left you in Crete, so that you might put what remained into order, and appoint *elders* in every town as I directed you." He goes further as he discusses the qualifications, but overseer and elder are listed interchangeably. Merkle continues to write,

> A similar usage is found in 1 Peter 5:1-2. Peter, as a fellow elder, exhorts the elders of the churches. He writes, "I exhort the *elders* among you, as a fellow elder... shepherd the flock of God that is among you, serving as *"overseers"* (my translation, emphasis added)." Although this example is not as definitive since the verb form (serving as overseers) is used (and not the noun overseers), it still emphasizes that the duty or function of the elders was to oversee the congregation. It would be strange if the elders

---

[117]Ibid., 19-20.

were not the same people as those who were called overseers since they both perform the same duties.[118]

The responsibility of the current or potential leader is often decided by the constitution of a church, which may not always align with the biblical precedent or even the denominational polity of the church. Conner writes, ". . . the duties of a church leader have eternal consequences. Leaders, especially pastors or elders, are not merely responsible for running an organization but have the crucial role of shepherding, teaching, and equipping the congregation. In addition, church leaders are examples to the rest of the flock."[119] Leaders are held to a higher standard of responsibility.

It is imperative to implement leadership from the biblical standpoint of governmental organization as the leaders have the responsibility of shepherding the congregation. Connor writes, "Leaders in the church (elders in particular) are given the task of making sure those in their charge have a healthy relationship with God." It should be an understanding that the calling of the church leader is not to promote secular growth but to empower their fellow brothers and sisters to seek the Great Shepherd.[120]

God calls shepherds to multiple responsibility. Conner writes, "But shepherds not only lead; they also must protect. In Acts 20, Paul warns the Ephesian elders that after he is gone, savage wolves will come in among them and

---

[118]Ibid., 20.

[119]Conner, 11-12.

[120]Ibid., 12.

will not spare the flock (v. 29). Godly church leaders are needed to shepherd the flock and to protect them against false teachers who would seek to lead the sheep astray." It is the responsibility of the leader to ensure that the sheep are safe.[121]

Those who are leaders also have a responsibility to ensure accurate information is disseminated or it could lead to a disastrous outcome. Harrington enlightens us in this regard, "Since the content of Christian faith is clear, Timothy the pastor must see that no different doctrine is taught (1:3) and that all hold to sound teaching (1:10). The mystery of faith is an objective thing to be held onto (3:9), and the church must function as the pillar and bulwark of the truth (3:15)." It is from the Pastorals that we get the idea of "the deposit of faith (6:20)."[122]

He also suggests, "The opposite of sound doctrine is meaningless talk (1:6), which proceeds from those who pay attention to deceitful spirits and teachings of demons (4:1). The opponents are fascinated by myths and genealogies (1:4) and forbid marriage and demand abstinence from certain foods (4:3). In the Pastorals, there is a clear line between the sound doctrines of the Pauline tradition and the false doctrines of the false teachers." 1 Timothy sets forth a more focused awareness that refutes the existence of church leaders who are teaching a falsified gospel. The minister of "biblical times became the authority in projecting the gospel and leading the flock according to sound doctrine. There is also an officially recognized order of widows with carefully

---

[121]Ibid.

[122]Daniel J. Harrington, *Who Is Jesus? Why Is He Important? An Invitation to the New Testament* (Sheed & Ward, Franklin, WI, 1999), 132-133.

prescribed entrance requirements (5:3-16). Finally, 5:17-22 lists rules for elders or presbyters concerning their salary, procedures to be followed when they are accused of sin, and their evaluation before ordination."[123]

It is clear that the leader has a vital role in protecting the doctrine of the church. Paul emphasizes to Timothy the responsibility of those who are in the positions of leadership. He charges him with the importance of holding fast to his instructions and the damage that could be done if instructions are not heeded. Paul was a good judge of character as he sent Timothy to Ephesus to instruct certain men about teaching false doctrine. Woolfe writes, "Paul knew that this assignment would force his young protégé to stretch, but he felt he had picked the right developmental assignment for him. He advised Timothy to stay in Ephesus, so that he may command certain men not to teach false doctrine any longer nor to devote themselves to myths and endless genealogies" (1 Tim 1:3-4).[124] Paul understood the assignment and continued to encourage the pastor, Timothy, as he fulfilled this arduous mandate (1 Tim 1:18-19).[125]

Likewise from Timothy to Titus, Paul continues to set up structure in Crete. Harrington continues to list instructions, "In Titus 1:5-9, Titus is charged with setting up church structures on the island of Crete. He is to appoint elders; he is to choose a bishop who is respected not only for his natural virtues but also for

---

[123]Ibid.

[124]Lorin Woolfe, *Leadership Secrets from the Bible.* New York, NY: Published by MJF Books, 2002, 205-206.

[125]Ibid., 206.

his firm grasp on the gospel and ability 'to preach with sound doctrine and to refute those who contradict it' (1:9). Titus himself is to teach, 'what is consistent with sound doctrine (2:1).'"[126]

In his book, *Early Christian Fathers,* Cyril Richardson discusses the leadership role of the bishop as it relates to its historical view. He writes,

> Under the single bishop who, with his council of presbyters, rules the congregation, there is built up a closely-knit organization, which will be able to withstand the concerted persecutions of the third century. The bishop is the successor of the apostles, representing the localizing of the prophetic, teaching, and liturgical functions of the original apostolate. He becomes the center of the Church's life, the living witness and guardian of its faith. Exactly how it came about that a single bishop should succeed to powers earlier vested in local bodies of presbyters, is not altogether clear; though much may be explained by the occasional settling of an apostle, prophet, or teacher of the original missionary ministry, in some locality. What, however, is clear is that the development was orderly, and that it was very widespread by the time of Ignatius. The obvious convenience of having a single administrative head, the economic necessity whereby a congregation could afford to maintain only one full-time official, the dominance of certain leading personalities, together with the suitability of having a single celebrant for worship-all these factors doubtless played a role in the rise of the monepiscopate. It is, indeed, already foreshadowed in the Pastoral Epistles, where Timothy and Titus are viewed as Paul's delegates, entrusted with the supervision of the presbyteries in Ephesus and Crete. The final step is taken in

---

[126]Harrington, 136.

the communities reflected in Ignatius' correspondence. There the bishop is the bishop of a local congregation, and the term originally synonymous with "presbyter," now characterizes this distinctive office.[127]

Ferguson writes, "The three-fold ministry of the local church (bishop, presbyters, deacons) became the general pattern by the mid-second century. The emergence of one bishop at the head of the presbyter (monepiscopacy) is attested first at Antioch of Syria and in Asia Minor by the letters of Ignatius. The bishop, as portrayed in the letters of Ignatius, was still a local bishop in a city (not territorial bishop), and nothing is said of apostolic succession or a priestly function."[128]

Ferguson also writes, "The bishop was assisted by presbyters as counselors, but especially by deacons, about whom more is said than about presbyters. There was also an order of widows, whose responsibility was primarily to pray, but not to teach or baptize, and an order of deaconesses, who ministered in the women's quarters of houses and gave the anointing and teaching to women at their baptism."[129]

There were two offices recognized in the church by the time the Pastoral Epistles (1-2 Tim, Ti) were written. They were overseers and deacons. Merkle writes,

---

[127] Cyril Richardson, *Early Christian Fathers* (Touchstone 1996), 20.

[128] Ferguson, 107.

[129] Ibid.

Yet, overseers and deacons also were mentioned in Paul's earlier letter to the Philippians. In his opening greeting, he addresses "all the saints in Christ Jesus who are at Philippi, with the overseers and deacons" (Phil 1:1). In 1 Timothy 3, Paul gives qualifications for the two offices. In verse 1 he writes, "If anyone aspires to the office of overseer, he desires a noble task." The following verses give the needed qualifications for those who might hold such an office. Then, in verse 8, Paul shifts to the office of deacon: Deacons likewise must . . . Paul's letter to Titus, however, refers only to overseers, making no mention of deacons (Ti 1:5-9). This omission possibly indicates that the church in Crete was less developed than the church in Ephesus.[130]

A "particular church order" was established by the "Apostolic Fathers." The interchangeable names of "elders or bishops" and deacons were recognized in each church structure namely:

1. Jerusalem and Judea-Acts 11:30; 15:6; James 5:14
2. Syria-*Didache* 15:1
3. Galatia-Acts 14:23
4. Asia Minor-1 Peter 5:1-4
5. Ephesus-Acts 20:17, 28; 1 Timothy 3:1-13
6. Philippi-Philippians 1:1; Polycarp, *Philippians* 6
7. Corinth-1 *Clement* 42:4; 44:3-6
8. Crete-Titus 1:5-7
9. Rome-*1 Clement* 42; 44; Hermas, *Vision* 3.5.1[131]

In the "Teaching of the Apostles, (The *Didascalia Apostolorum*)," it was noted that the bishop was set aside as the "teacher and preacher, moral watchman,

---

[130]Ibid., 18-19.

[131]Ibid.

judge in cases of discipline, pastor who seeks the lost sheep, and spiritual physician healing sick souls who repent" and the lead person of the "local church." He was also the one responsible for overseeing the possessions of the church, by "which he, the clergy, and the poor were supported." His duties further included, as "the administrator of baptism, anointing, and eucharist and the church's priest (offering spiritual sacrifices)." He was accountable as the general overseer in all matters of the church.[132]

We assume that we are familiar with whom may be a Christian by the confession of one's faith or even by referring to them as brothers or sisters in the Lord, but God is the only One who can determine who actually belongs to His family (2 Tim 2:19). This means that anyone from any walk of life or background can receive forgiveness through the death and resurrection of Jesus Christ; this is commonly called the universal church which is comprised of a variety of local churches with different people who congregate regularly for the purpose of teaching, fellowship, and worship.[133] Paul wrote letters to the local churches in cities such as Philippi, Corinth, Ephesus, Colossae, and Thessalonica to bring order and structure to the church and to convey the way for them to live Christian lives as the body of Christ.[134]

---

[132]Ibid., 173.

[133]Driscoll, 11.

[134]Ibid., 12.

The apostle Paul was very instrumental in giving pastoral charge to specific community members and instructions to the church in Thessalonica to inform them of their leadership structure and to whom they would be held accountable "(Ro 12:6 - *proistameno*)." According to Acts 14:22, there were presbyters appointed to leadership in every local church by apostles Barnabas and Paul when they launched out on their first missionary journey. According to the Catholic Encyclopedia, in her writings of, *The Church*, Joyce George writes, ". . . in the account of Paul's interview with the Ephesian elders (Acts 20:17-23), it is told that, sending from Miletus to Ephesus, he summoned the presbyters of the Church, and in the course of his charge addressed them as follows: 'Take heed to yourselves and to the whole flock, wherein the Holy Ghost has placed you bishops to tend [*poimainein*] the Church of God (20:28).'" Joyce George discusses further the evidence of the presbyters authority as she continues to write, "The presbyters that are among you, . . . tend [*poimainein*] the flock of God which is among you . . . The Epistle of St. James provides us with yet another reference to this office, where the sick man is bidden to send for the presbyters of the Church, that he may receive at their hands the rite of unction (Jas 5:14)." This is where the elders of the Church are called to lay hands on the sick in order for them to recover from their infirmity.[135]

Joyce George further writes,

> It remains to consider whether the so-called monarchical episcopate was instituted by the Apostles. Besides

---

[135] Joyce George, *The Church*, The Catholic Encyclopedia. Vol. 3. New York, NY: Robert Appleton Company, 1908, 30 Apr. 2012 http://www.newadvent.org/cathen/03744a.htm.

establishing a college of presbyter-bishops, did they further place one man in a position of supremacy, entrusting the government of the Church to him, and endowing him with apostolic authority over the Christian community? Even if we take into account the Scriptural evidence alone, there are sufficient grounds for answering this question in the affirmative. From the time of the dispersion of the Apostles, St. James appears in an episcopal relation to the Church of Jerusalem (Acts 12:17; 15:13; Gal 2:12). In the other Christian communities the institution of monarchical bishops was a somewhat later development. At first the Apostles themselves fulfilled, it would seem, all the duties of supreme oversight. They established the office when the growing needs of the Church demanded it. The Pastoral Epistles leave no room to doubt that Timothy and Titus were sent as bishops to Ephesus and to Crete respectively. To Timothy full Apostolic powers are conceded. Notwithstanding his youth he holds authority over both clergy and laity. To him is confided the duty of guarding the purity of the Church's faith, of ordaining priests, of exercising jurisdiction. Moreover, St. Paul's exhortation to him, "to keep the commandment without spot, blameless, unto the coming of our Lord Jesus Christ" shows that this was no transitory mission. A charge so worded includes in its sweep, not Timothy alone, but his successors in an office, which is to last until the Second Advent. Local tradition unhesitatingly reckoned him among the occupants of the episcopal see. At the Council of Chalcedon, the Church of Ephesus counted a succession of twenty-seven bishops commencing with Timothy.[136]

---

[136]Ibid.

One item that is more important than bearing any title would be the reputation of the leader, whether they are an elder, deacon, overseer, pastor or bishop. It is not a far cry that many leaders have fallen prey to damaging situations that put a stain on Christianity. True checks and balances must be set in place to protect not only the leader but also the congregants. Mark Driscoll discusses the steps that would assist a leader to stay pure and beyond reproach. Driscoll writes,

> First, a leader must fear God and be accountable to him. Simply, if any Christian, including a pastor, does not fear God and walk closely with Jesus, then there is truly nothing that can be done to keep him or her [guard, against, protect] in an evil manner. Second, leaders must be accountable to their spouse if they are married. No one knows how we are doing better than our spouse. Third, a leader must be accountable to other leaders in close relationships marked by honest answers to tough questions. Among the elders this also means that our wives are close and are given the freedom to speak openly about the condition of their marriages and homes with one another so that there is never any hiding of sin among our elder teams. Fourth, leaders must be in good relations with the leaders of other godly churches in their area to practice unity on the local level as a witness to the city about the unity of God's people. Fifth, leaders must also respect whatever additional accountability structures are needed, including denominational leadership, personal life coaching, or a biblical counselor.[137]

---

[137]Driscoll, 76.

Let us take a look at the roles that served the church according to the leadership structure in Philippians 1:1; elders, deacons, and church members. Each of these leadership roles was accountable for the health and progress of what was called the local church. The Scripture addresses the saints, overseers and deacons at Philippi. First, there are elders (overseers in this verse), who are the senior leadership in the church. Second, there are deacons, who function as pastoral assistants by also leading the church alongside the elders. Third, there are saints, or Christians, who love God and help lead the local church by using their resources (time, talent, and treasure) to help build up their church as church members.[138]

As we look further at the discussion on leadership, we cannot negate the opportunity to first define church. Mark Driscoll writes, "The church is the community of all Christians throughout history who have been loved and saved by Jesus Christ, (Acts 20:28; Eph 5:25), including the believing people of the Old Testament. (Dt 4:10; Acts 7:38; Heb 2:12; cf. Ps 22:22). In every church, there are people who are not Christians, (Mt 13:24-30) including both lost people and wolves sent by Satan to lead people astray. (Acts 20:29-30)."

There are times that leaders are mentioned in the New Testament that are not given any titles at all. In Galatians 6:6, Paul states, "One who is taught the word must share all good things with the one who teaches." In other words, it is the responsibility of those receiving instruction to provide for the physical sustenance of their teachers. "This verse suggests that there was a class of

---

[138]Ibid., 13.

instructors or catechizers who taught the word to such an extent that they needed to be financially supported for their work." Also, in 1 Thessalonians 5:12-13, Paul exhorts the congregation: "We ask you, brothers, to respect those who labor among you, and are over you in the Lord and admonish you; and to esteem them very highly in love because of their work." There is an order that Paul suggests the brothers to adhere with regard to those responsible for teaching the masses. Both passages of Scripture insinuate a position of leadership, but there is no official title given to the mentioned leaders.[139]

In Hebrews, the distinction is made between those who were selected as leaders and those who are given the instructions to obey those leaders: "Obey your leaders and submit to them, for they are keeping watch over your souls, as those who will have to give an account" (Heb 13:17). Connor states, "What could be a more important and, at the same time, a more frightening job description?"[140] Benjamin L. Merkle writes, "If a leader must give an account, he needs to know not only that he is a leader (which implies some formal position recognized by the church) but also who he is accountable to lead (which implies a distinction between the leaders and the followers)." Although we do not know what particular office these leaders may have held, we do know that the author has in mind a distinct group of individuals. It is also possible that this passage alluded to those who were considered New Testament pastors.[141]

---

[139]Merkle, 18.

[140]Connor, 12.

[141]Ibid., 18.

Deacons

It is traditionally observed by the church that the origin of the office of deacon developed in Acts 6, when the seven men were chosen to assist the twelve. However, it is not recorded that the name deacon was bestowed upon that group of men although they provided "daily ministration," *diakonia*, the work of a servant, service of believers. The word for deacon, *diakonos,* is never used in this passage, only the character of the work of a servant is mentioned. Connor writes, "there is no positive proof that this was the origin of the office of a deacon."[142] Let us take a more detailed look at this passage of Scripture for further analysis:

> Now in these days when the disciples were increasing in number, a complaint by the Hellenists arose against the Hebrews because their widows were being neglected in the daily distribution. And the twelve summoned the full number of the disciples and said, "It is not right that we should give up preaching the word of God to serve tables. Therefore, brothers, pick out from among you seven men of good repute, full of the Spirit and of wisdom, whom we will appoint to this duty. But we will devote ourselves to prayer and to the ministry of the word." And what they said pleased the whole gathering, and they chose Stephen, a man full of faith and of the Holy Spirit, and Philip, and Prochorus, and Nicanor, and Timon, and Parmenas, and Nicolaus, a proselyte of Antioch. These they set before the apostle, and they prayed and laid their hands on them. And the word of God continued to increase, and the number of the disciples multiplied greatly in Jerusalem, and a great many of the priests became obedient to the faith.[143]

---

[142] Ibid., 264.

[143] Acts 6:1-7.

The positive circumstance of the passage is that the Kingdom of God was increasing and expanding because of the preaching of the word. However, along with growth comes growing pangs of providing congregational care for a larger congregation of people. One group of people felt that their "widows were being neglected in the daily distribution." This type of circumstance is also evident in modern day churches; the pastors (including all leaders who are tasked to preach the Gospel) are unfairly inundated with providing congregational care simply to fulfill a job description. If this method is followed it is likely that parts of the congregation may be inadvertently overlooked. It is with this thought that the apostles understood their role in the church and knew that their preaching of the Gospel was superior to their serving tables. They solicited all of the disciples to select a group of seven men to handle this particular business. The criterion for this specific duty was: must be of good repute; full of the Spirit; and of wisdom. For this task, they appointed Stephen, who would soon after be martyred; Philip the evangelist; Prochorus; Nicanor; Timon, Parmenas, and Nicolas a proselyte of Antioch, all who theologians declared in historical writings, were later appointed as bishops of various provinces.[144]

With the resolution of this issue, the "word of God continued to increase and disciples multiplied greatly" because the apostles were able to preach while the seven ensured that everyone was receiving their distributional proportions. Although the apostles laid hands on them to carry out this mission, the latter four were never mentioned again in the Scriptures handling any further business. Thus,

---

[144]Ibid.

this specific service did not appear to be a permanent position for the seven. These findings suggests that the Acts 6 moment of service was just that, a specific service offered for a temporary period of time as the seven men each went on to other assignments. This premise diminishes the claim that any position, appointed or voted in, is a required lifetime commitment or responsibility.

In addition, Paul listed the qualifications for deacon, *diakonos,* found in 1 Timothy 3:8-10 is: they must be dignified (honorable), not double-tongued (not a liar), not addicted to much wine (not a drunk), not greedy for dishonest gain (not a thief), must hold the mystery of the faith with a clear conscience and they must be tested first then they can serve as a deacon if they proved themselves, be the husband of one wife, managing their children and their own households well. Paul gave these practical qualifications which are frequently overlooked in the church today. Often times the people that are appointed to this position possess qualities that Paul prohibits.

It should be noted that service does not have a gender. However, the culture in the early church was that of male domination of leadership roles and women subject only to household chores. There are many who try to differentiate *diakonos* as deacon for males and deaconess for females, because there are various conflicts involving females having any leadership roles in the church. However, Paul lists a description for men as deacons in 1 Timothy 3:8-10, but transitions to discuss the characteristics of yet another "type" of deacon. Many writings refer to this section as the description for the female deacon. Ironically, there is not a standard for the wives of the pastor/bishop listed in the previous versus, so why would Paul decide at this point to address wives of deacons in the middle of a description for a deacon if the wives were not a part of the same genre? As the eleventh verse starts, it says, "Even so *(hosautos)* wives be . . ." suggests that their wives are, likewise, in like manner, even as the former was that the latter shall be. Consequently, Paul addressed Phoebe as a *diakonos* (Ro 16:1), which is the same word usage for a male deacon; there was no distinction between male and female service *(diakonos)* in Greek as Paul used the same word to describe Phoebe as her male counterparts who were *diakonos.* Although other deacons rendered service in the church, Phoebe was the one responsible for the delivery of the Epistle to the Church at Rome and was also considered a succourer *(prostatis) a* protectress, "wealthy patron" or a leader among many (Ro 16:2). In the early church, people who held the title *Prostates* held great responsibility over the welfare of people who did not have civil rights.[145]

> Consider the following:
>
> The major issue here is that no specific word for wife (or husband) is to be found in the Koine, the Greek in which all books of our New Testament were written. The only unequivocal way to designate a wife was to speak of the woman of a certain person. Where that designation is lacking, as in the current passage, it becomes a judgment call as to whether wife is meant, or simply a woman.
>
> In order to properly set this in context, we need to begin with the opening verses of Chapter 3. From 3:2 to 3:8, the qualifications for an overseer ("bishop") are set forth. In 3:8 the phrase "deacons (likewise)" would appear to indicate that the qualifications for bishop would also apply to deacons. Then some further qualifications for being a

---

[145] Vines, 147, 208.

deacon are contained here. With v. 11 the phrase "(women likewise)" appears. Now, if the proper translation is "wives," whose wives are they? By this point in the text both bishops and deacons have been mentioned and their qualifications spelled out. Are only the wives of deacons or bishops significant enough to be called upon to have these specific qualifications? This would make no sense, it seems to me. For one thing, the author could have made things crystal clear by adding "(of deacons)" or "(of bishops)"-or both, after the word "women," had he intended to refer to wives of either or both groups. Since he did not do so, I take it that this is not what he meant. I believe he was thinking about women in the same or similar positions as the bishops and deacon. The parallel way in which he introduces deacons and women would seem to support this conclusion. Furthermore, if wives of deacons were intended, why would he list part of the qualifications for deacons, then qualifications for their wives, then finalize his list of qualifications for deacons? If the women in similar positions were to be held to the same high standards as the male deacons, then this makes perfect sense.[146]

In order to fairly discuss the "husband of one wife" *(Mias gunaikos andra),* represented the devotion of a husband to his wife, a "one-woman man" in heart and soul. This passage deals with the character of pastors/bishops and deacons, it then compares the characteristics of "wives" *(gune),* meaning a woman who is either married or unmarried with that of the former for men.[147]

---

[146] Joe E. Lunceford, *Women Likewise: A Closer Look at 1 Timothy 3:11,* Religion Department Georgetown College, March 2011. Bibleinterp.com/opeds/womlik358015.shtml.

[147] Andreas Kostenberger, *Biblical Foundations, Women Deacons,* April 24, 2006 in Blog.

This definition of the word "wives" would have little to any reference to how a woman can be the "husband of one wife." She cannot nor would she as a woman in service of this culture would most likely not be married but would be dedicated completely to the service of God which makes v. 12 non-applicable to her service but not a disqualification of her status as a *diakonos*.[148] This verse and others similar to it that suppresses the leadership role of women is based more on a cultural position instead of a theological perspective. In light of the context of the original language my supposition would be that of support and the existence of deacons who are female.[149] Although Scripture is in support of female deacons, it is strictly at the discretion of the church if this belief would be a benefit to the ministry, seeing that there is often a lack of male attendees.

In addition to the former, 1 Timothy 3:8, states that the qualifications of a deacon were closely related with the functions of pastors/bishops, which were for spiritual resolves, with the exceptions of being apt to teach and taking care of the church of God (1 Tim 3:2 & 5). The exceptions are indicative of the level of authority that the pastor/bishop has over the office of the deacon as there is no requirement for deacons to teach or rule the church.

The primary function of a deacon is neither to teach nor to rule but to provide service to others for the Kingdom of God as an assistant to the under shepherd. Today, the duties of the deacon are traditionally mislabeled to be responsible for the business and financial affairs of the church. This does not

---

[148] Bible.org/question/will.

[149] Vines, 681.

insinuate that a man should be given the office of deacon solely because his business skills are impeccable. Rather, his moral and spiritual behavior should far outweigh his ability to handle business and financial affairs before he uses the office of a deacon.[150]

It is to this end that the position titles of trustee (building & grounds/fiduciary accountability), Director of Christian Education (church education responsibility), secretary (communications distribution), church clerk (manage church records), etc . . . are not biblical roles of the church but are man-made titles instituted by the church on the basis of need - *not to lead the church*. Even though in some cases having a trustee is a requirement of the state, it is absolutely necessary that the person(s) selected to serve should equally be Spirit-led as are the other positions of need. It is a horrendous injustice to have someone over the communications, education, financial offerings and monies of the church, which is not Spirit-led. While the role of a deacon is biblical, it still does not have the authority to usurp the under shepherd. Therefore, it is ascribed that neither of these positions qualifies any individual to rule the under shepherd of the church. God will honor the person He has set in place to lead - not those who are self-appointed because of seniority, secular gifts or know-how.

Consequently, leaders must be true followers of Jesus Christ in order to accomplish the successes of leadership. This will encourage other people to follow them as they follow Jesus. This will dictate the necessity of church leaders becoming exemplary followers who follow their Chief Shepherd Jesus before they

---

[150]Ibid., 264-265.

become leaders of any group, organization or church. In 1 Corinthians 11:1, Paul instructed the local churches to follow him, as he is an imitator of Christ. Driscoll writes, "While it may seem obvious to insist that any discussion of church leadership begin with the centrality and preeminence of Jesus, sadly, many churches omit Him from their organizational charts altogether. At the risk of stating the obvious, every church must place Jesus Christ in the position of Highest Authority and devotion in both the organizational chart and the life of the church." It is necessary to the existence of the church that Jesus is seen as the Headship and is responsible for guiding her to purpose.[151]

Even though Paul wrote letters addressing many churches, he was neither the Head nor the One to set the standards. Mark Driscoll writes, "The Scriptures are clear that Jesus Christ is the Head of the Church (Eph 1:9, 22-23; 4:15; 5:23). Jesus is the Apostle who plants a church (Heb 3:1). Jesus is the Leader who builds the church (Mt 16:18). Jesus is the Senior Pastor and Chief Shepherd who rules the church (1 Pt 5:4), and it is ultimately Jesus who closes churches down when they have become faithless or fruitless (Rev 2:5)." It is to this end that we must acknowledge Jesus as the "go to" for church leadership. Driscoll, writes, "Therefore, it is absolutely vital that a church loves Jesus, obeys Jesus, imitates Jesus, and follows Jesus at all times and in all ways, according to the teaching of his word (Col 3:16)."[152] Jesus is the Leader to follow.

---

[151]Ibid., 12.

[152]Ibid.

CHAPTER 4

Leading Effectively

Spiritual leadership is different from secular leadership. One can employ spiritual leadership in a secular environment; however secular leadership cannot always be employed in a spiritual environment. Therefore, a Christian leader is one that is chosen and led by the Holy Spirit. In his book *The Leader Within*, Michael Thomas Scott eloquently writes, "It is imperative that God's leaders develop a life of consecration and spiritual discipline. The nourishment of the inner life is absolutely necessary for liberating the 21st century leader within. Nothing can ever replace the spiritual benefits and blessings of having a personal relationship with Christ . . . God has chosen you for such a time as this, but one must now consider the process of consecration for meaningful leadership."[153] Without character development, it will be difficult to effectively lead others. The following examples from Scripture relate at least six ways to effectively lead:

Give an example for others – If you want to build people, they must have an example. Leadership begins with the example's life. An individual cannot take a person beyond where they have been themselves. Be a model of what you want others to be. Jesus never asked anyone to do anything that He had not already done and was already doing. John 13:15 states, "I've given you an

---

[153]Scott, 28.

example to follow. Now do as I have done to you." Jesus is saying here, "I did it, now you do it." He modeled servanthood.[154]

Challenge others for good – People should be positively challenged to a greater purpose. Leaders help others to see beyond themselves. They point the focus toward thinking in a bigger way. Because it is easy to live a self-centered life, leaders tend to focus on a greater cause, and a grander purpose. Jesus gave the young rich ruler a challenge that exposed his priorities. In Mark 10:21, Jesus says, "Go, sell everything you have and give to the poor, and you will have treasure in heaven. Then come follow me." He promised something better than wealth.[155]

Encourage others – Their potential should be affirmed. If you want to affirm the potential of others, treat them the way they are to become not the way they are. When someone believes in the potential of another it causes the individual to be encouraged and can bring the best out of them. They should know that they are important, they are valued and they matter. In John 14:12, Jesus says "Anyone who has faith in Me will do what I have been doing. He will do even greater things than these, because I am going to the Father." Jesus modeled this.[156]

Offer others honest feedback – Occasional correction is often needed. A negative must always be followed by a positive. That is how honest feedback is

---

[154] Jn 13:15.

[155] Mk 10:21.

[156] Jn 14:12.

given. Matthew 17:19-20 states, "Then the disciples came to Jesus in private and asked, 'Why couldn't we drive it out?'" He replied, 'Because you have so little faith. Truly I tell you, if you have faith as small as a mustard seed, you can say to this mountain, "Move from here to there," and it will move.'"[157] Jesus gave correction without condemning His potential leaders.

Treat others as equal – Real leaders do not act superior. They do not try to outshine those they lead. They purpose to treat everyone the same. Treating others as equal means that the leader accepts the responsibility but shares the credit with everybody. In John 15:15, Jesus says, "I no longer call you servants, because a servant does not know his master's business. Instead I have called you friends, for everything that I learned from my Father I have made known to you."[158] Jesus modeled sharing.

Pray much for others – Employers should pray for their employees, teachers should pray for their students, pastors should pray for their members, parents for their children and leaders for those they lead. Luke 22:32 states, "But I have prayed for you, Simon, that your faith may not fail. And when you have turned back, strengthen your brothers." Jesus expects His leaders to do likewise.

These six ways to effectively lead are for people building and development. It is beneficial to invest in people, not simply to receive from them but to galvanize them to rise to their fullest potential. If leaders give an example for others, challenge others for good, encourage others, offer others honest

---

[157]Mt 17:19-20.

[158]Jn 15:15.

feedback, treat others as equal and pray much for others, then there will be an impact on the church at large and then current and potential leaders will be empowered.

Effectively Leading Through Prayer

In the New Testament, prayer has been deemed a vital part of the duties of the ministerial leader. It adds value to the responsibility of the preacher as his/her responsibilities continue after he or she leaves the pulpit. In *The Ability of God: Prayers of the Apostle Paul,* Arthur W. Pink writes, "The preacher's obligations are not fully discharged when he leaves the pulpit, for he needs to water the seed he has sown. It has already been seen that the apostles devoted themselves 'continually to prayer, and to the ministry of the word,' and therein have they left an excellent example to be observed by all who follow them in the sacred vocation." The lack of sincere prayer can cause the sermon of a preacher to be unctionless to the hearers. One should labor in prayer before God in order to effectively convey His message to the masses. Arthur Pink writes, "Unless the sermon is the product of earnest prayer, we must not expect it to awaken the Spirit of prayer in those who hear it." The preacher has an obligation to travail in prayer in private to ask God to protect the word in the hearts of the hearer in order to bear fruit to God's eternal praise.[159]

---

[159]Arthur W. Pink. *The Ability of God: Prayers of the Apostle Paul* (Chicago, IL: The Moody Bible Institute of Chicago, 1967, 2000), 15.

The medium for spiritual communication is prayer to God in order to receive directions for the empowerment of the masses. Arthur W. Pink writes, "We must be in tune with God before we are fitted to go forth and speak in His name."

The people of Colossae were reminded that their leaders were "always laboring fervently for them in prayers, so they may be able to stand perfect and complete in all the will of God (4:12)."[160] The leaders did not neglect to continuously pray to strengthen their spiritual fortitude.

Prayer is a conversation with God on the behalf of others and self. Janet S. Helme writes, "Prayer may very well be *the most important thing* a leader does when using these resources. Prayer is to *The Inviting Word* as detailed blueprints are to a church building. Leaders who begin their preparation time with prayer, who pray at times during the process, who pray for their learners during every week, and who encourage the learners to pray for one another can expect to experience amazing things!"[161] Prayer releases Spirit-led results.

To pray to an unseen entity is an accomplishment of trust and a relinquishing of one's will. It is the giving of one's strength of character to receive the desires of the greater power, which is God. Timothy Jones discusses how one can relinquish themselves in prayer. He writes, "There is another way. While we say, 'Lord, this is what I want,' we also do not get too tied to the final answer. We press into God not with just desire but with open-ended trust. Not

---

[160] Ibid., 15-16.

[161] ucc.org/assets/pdfs/606LearnPray.pdf.

only with longing but also with hope."[162] The desire of God should be the desire of the one who enters into prayer.

Jones points out how writer Macrina Wiederkehr makes a distinction along these lines as she writes, "Rather than pray for the things she needs, she has begun to pray about them. 'When I pray for something,' she writes, 'my prayer tends to be much narrower. I put expectations on God. I expect something definite to happen and I am disappointed if it doesn't happen . . . I focus on the presence of God in my specific problem and we look at it together, God and I.'" When we pray, we pray with the purpose of receiving in faith, believing it is done. We anticipate that the One who hears will do what is right by us; either way, the prayer is answered. Our prayer is directed not so much to the provision as to the Provider. A leader who waits to receive direction from God is a leader worth following.[163]

Trusting God through prayer exemplifies that all decisions should be presented to Him. Jones writes, "Until recently my friend Jan Senn worked as a magazine editor in a Chicago suburb. A harassing neighbor at her apartment building drove her to live in a motel for several weeks while she searched for another place she could afford. 'But I kept running up against closed doors,' she wrote me. "So I finally realized that instead of presenting God with three options I could live with, I needed to ask God what he wanted me to do. I got to the point

---

[162]Timothy Jones, *The Art of Prayer: A Simple Guide to Conversation with God* (Colorado Springs, CO: WaterBrook Press, 2005), 214.

[163]Ibid.

where I was able to say to God, 'whatever,' that became her prayer of relinquishment." The prayers of a leader should display that they have a relationship of trust in God for His guidance.[164]

Jones writes, "Praying, for the believer therefore, is a choice that is made on the behalf of the one who is praying to trust if this expression of belief will truly realize transformation." When a leader spends time in prayer, it is a transformative event that simply cannot be explained except as a walk of faith with Someone who is only spiritually visible. Jones writes, "Most of us want to find a way of praying that gives our lives richness and hope. When we talk to God, can we do better than stammer? Can we move beyond rote repetition or stale habit? Is it possible to pray with confidence? Can time spent with God transform us?" Prayer brings an overall fulfillment that one can find solace and empowerment.[165]

James Griffiss asserts in his book, *A Silent Path to God,* "The context of belief in which we pray and in which we are met by the will of God means that there is a situation of trust or confidence in Another. But trust and confidence in Another are not things that simply happen, nor are they usually total and complete. When leaders enter earnestly into prayer and enter into the presence of God, this will lead to growth in trust and confidence, to grow in the belief that God performs in his life." Sometimes we may believe that God has left us alone and we feel that He will not respond to the prayers that we have prayed. However,

---

[164]Ibid., 214-215.

[165]Jones, 5.

we must shake the idea that God has forsaken us and focus on the necessity of prayer, which will generate empowerment, growth and transmutation.[166]

Many times our prayers are produced out of what we need from God. Timothy Jones writes,

> The things that stimulate us to turn to God may bring peace once we believe He is listening. When we pray we meet a God of inexhaustible resources that is when we feel a bit at ease. Prayer opens our immediate view. We pray hard for a child (very hard if the child is *ours*) going into surgery or in a major dilemma. We pray to stay employed. We pray for money. We pray to pass an exam. Once in God's presence, we also stay open to whatever he may do or show us.

Leaders should ultimately feel the need to pray for the empowerment to lead others.[167]

Prayer is an essential part of a believer's spiritual defense mechanism against the adversary. Dr. Geoffrey Guns expresses his thoughts as he writes,

> Prayer is the most important and potent spiritual weapon at our disposal. We are engaged in a spiritual conflict and we cannot deal with the power of the evil one purely on the wings of our feeble strength. We need and must use the weapons of our warfare as Paul pointed out in the book of 2 Corinthians 10:3-4, 'For though we walk in the flesh, we do not war according to the flesh, for the weapons of our warfare are not of the flesh, but divinely powerful for the destructions of fortresses.' Without the weapon of prayer,

---

[166]James E. Griffiss, *A Silent Path to God* (Philadelphia, PA: Fortress Press, 1980), 56.

[167]Jones, 24.

we will become casualties on the battlefield of life (Eph 6:18).[168]

Therefore, prayer should be the basis as leader empowerment evolves. Jesus understood the centrality of prayer. For example, Jesus frequently isolated Himself in order to pray. He gives example by separating from the masses to accomplish this mission. This suggestion of isolation perhaps places an emphasis on the importance of prayer. Mark 1:35 highlights the intention of Jesus to isolate Himself from the masses to communicate with God, "Very early in the morning, while it was still dark, Jesus got up, left the house and went off to a solitary place, where he prayed." There was an obvious importance as the possibility of interruption was minimized.[169]

In 1 Timothy 2:1, Paul encourages four types of prayers to Timothy. They are: supplications (petitioning), prayers (personalizing), intercessions (pleading), and thanksgivings (praising). These are important prayers to empower leaders.

1. *Petitioning* – making request to God.
2. *Personalizing* – tailor making the prayer to the need.
3. *Pleading* – beseeching God on the behalf of others.
4. *Praising* – giving thanks and blessings to God [170]

---

[168]Geoffrey V. Guns, *Cultivating the Discipline of Prayer: The Key to Having Power with God* (Norfolk, VA: 2005), 2.

[169]Mk 1:35.

[170]Tyree, Sermon.

Prayers are prayed to God for various things and He should be the only One impressed by one's prayer. Too often in public prayer, people structure their prayers to sound good to the hearer. They cross every "T" and dot every "I" as if they are looking for the approval of mankind instead of an answer from God. Some leaders are taught to use voice inflection at a specific time in the prayer and some even holler to the top of their voice as if God has a hearing challenge. Sometimes prayers sound rehearsed and repetitious because of a traditional mindset of the individual who perhaps has heard someone else approach prayer that way.

Let us understand that God is the only One that responds to our prayers and should be the One whom our prayers should be addressed. It is my belief that God is not concerned about our grammar, diction or voice inflection during prayer – it is the condition of the heart and sincere intentions (Lk 18:14). We can receive answers to prayer when we commit ourselves to His Gospel and turn our thoughts and hearts towards His purpose.[171]

It is also observed that in order to begin any project one should spend time in prayer for guidance as it is considered communication with God and has been proven to be an antidote to all of the ills of the world. Michael Scott states in *The Leader Within,*

> What is prayer all about? There are many different definitions for this one word "prayer." I have selected one very simple explanation of what prayer is all about as it relates to our discourse on liberating the leader within

---

[171] E. M. Bounds, *The Weapon of Prayer* (Grand Rapids, MI: Baker Book House, 1975), 40.

through the consecrated life. Stormie Omartian and Jack Hayford in their book, *The Power of Praying Together,* define prayer simply as 'communicating with God. Each time we pray, we come in contact with God in a profound and life-changing way.' As a 21st century leader, I have found that prayer provides the connection with the Divine that I need to encounter and experience the profound presence of God that brings about personal renewal for each day.[172]

Dr. Terry Thomas in his book, *Let Us Pray,* expounds upon the Spirit of prayer:

A strong illustration of what it means to have a constant sense of God's presence (the Spirit of prayer) can be seen in the relationship that exists between a police station and the officers on patrol. Police officers on patrol are not always in continuous conversation with the radio dispatcher at the police station although they are always in tune with each other. The officers know that if there is a need to make contact with the station, or if the watch commander needs to contact the officers, the officers can simply press a button to talk to the dispatcher at the station. Likewise, Christians are always connected with God through Jesus Christ. This allows us to always have a sense of God's presence.[173]

We are encouraged to pray in our spirits without stopping to take a break (1 Thes 5:16-18). To some, this may sound like a difficult task but it will quickly become a lifestyle of the individual; it is a discipline that a leader should

---

[172] Scott, 32-33.

[173] Terry Thomas, *Let Us Pray*, 13.

incorporate in their daily routine as it will be difficult to lead effectively without a commitment to prayer. Prayer in general should be a practice no matter what the circumstances may be. This is the way God wants those who belong to Christ Jesus to live. Even though we may not have our eyes closed, be able to kneel down or lay prostrate before God, we can still talk to Him anytime and He in turn will respond according to His desire. We must ensure that our hearts remain open to hear what God will share.

The apostle Paul was clearly a man of prayer. It was an obvious key to the success that he experienced during the many years of his ministry (Acts 16:19). Many of the prayers of the apostle have been preserved in his letters to the various churches that he wrote. From his writing in the New Testament, a great deal about Paul's life was engulfed in prayer. When leaders pray, they receive clear revelation of themselves.

We should strive to know God through prayer as we will then begin to know who we are in Him. "So prayer is an intensively human experience in which our eyes are opened and we begin to see more clearly our true nature." Therefore, time spent in prayer is not wasted time and it will also keep the vision of one's being sharp enough to flow in Christian leadership.[174]

Prayer requires faith on the behalf of the one entering into prayer. As we read in Hebrews, God demands faith to be incorporated in our prayers because without faith on our part, pleasing God would be impossible (Heb 11:6). Jesus

---

[174]Kenneth Leech, *True Prayer: An Invitation To Christian Spirituality* (San Francisco, CA: Harper and Row Publishers, 1980), 3.

instructs us to have faith in God even if we do not see the manifestation of His handiwork immediately. We are instructed to live by our faith not by what we see in the natural (2 Cor 5:7) while we wait on the manifestation of what we have requested. We should believe that we have received whatever our prayer is concerning. As a leader, we should exhibit faith in God to know He has answered all our prayers according to His word. If we have any doubt, we should not expect anything. Our prayers should be prayers of faith versus prayers that have partial doubt which would be prayers prayed in vain. Leaders should be people of faith as they pray and expect the impossible to manifest.

Accordingly, when God speaks His word to us, it causes us to be God-centered instead of self-centered. This process becomes crucial for Christian leaders, as we believe and our total being is centered on God. The word will keep the leader centered in God as it is spoken and believed. It is then that the leader can focus on the mission and not the man.[175]

Many prayers of confession, thanksgiving and grace were prayed by fathers and mothers of the faith. There were leaders of the church who communicated to God through prayer. Martin Luther understood the need for a leader to have a prayer agenda. He was known to say, "There are three things which go to the making of a successful preacher: supplication, meditation, and tribulation. This was taken down by one of his students from his Table Talks. We are not sure the exact meaning that the great Reformer, Martin Luther, purposed, but we assume that he meant that prayer is essential to bring the leader

---

[175]Leech, 3.

(messenger) into a suitable frame to understand divine things and endue him with power as prayer opens a channel to the Divine that is otherwise closed in the natural."[176]

Leaders should also be encouraged not only to pray for their learners but also for their counterparts in the ministry. Paul Elbert writes, "In a letter to the respected cardinal Sadoleto, Calvin enjoined in prayer for the Lord to grant the only true bond of ecclesiastical unity . . . through His one word and Spirit, that we might join together with one heart and one soul. The church today is still moving toward that vital goal, with ample weight being given to the unity of the Spirit and the potential unity of the faith (Eph 4:3, 13)." This would promote unity among the leadership as each aims to work meritoriously for the Kingdom.[177]

Dealing with Conflict

It is observed that in any project that involves more than two people, there will be some form of conflict as people tend to have a difference of opinion about any one point. Amos 3 asks the question, "Do two walk together unless they have agreed to do so?" Some may even go as far to say that at least one of the individuals is simply a difficult person and will cause a rift in any situation because of their character. Sometimes that may be the case however, as Christian leaders our job is to suppress the conflict at the minimum level.

Conflict is a major component of leadership. It is impossible to be a leader and not face some sort of opposition. What exactly is conflict? Merriam-Webster

---

[176]Pink, 15.

[177]Elbert, *Calvin and the Spiritual Gift*, 256.

writes, conflict is: "the opposition of persons or forces that gives rise to the dramatic action."[178] It is with this definition that we will surround our discussion.

Who has time to deal with conflict when there is so much work to be done and so many lives to be transformed? Whether internal or external, conflict has a way of slowing progress. In some cases, conflict can totally annihilate a mission or plan unless one has learned how to work in, work with, or work around it. It is presupposed that all would desire the same peaceful atmosphere as everyone strives to accomplish a single goal as a united body. However, we are far from a perfect world. Even though many may be on the same team, it should be understood that a team spirit does not always dwell among the team.

It is unfortunate, but conflict simply cannot be avoided. It can be the driving force to a divided church or a springboard to improve practices, processes and procedures of a church. It can also amplify weaknesses that may exist in individuals that are involved. Dr. Terry Thomas writes, ". . . strangely, just as a conflict can disrupt and terribly rupture a church, a conflict can also be good for a church, a ministry or an organization. In and of itself, a conflict is not necessarily bad. The absence of conflict may be an indication of the lack of health."[179] Jesus lets us know that we should expect offences to come but He gives a process for resolving the conflict that arises (Mt 18:7, 15-17).

Some leaders may have a challenge confronting issues head on, as they feel inadequate dealing with conflict because of fear. The fear of facing

---

[178]Merriman-Webster: *Conflict*.

[179]Terry Thomas – lecture notes, 91.

opposition should not be an excuse to avoid dealing with issues because of the possible chaotic aftermath. If the conflict is not timely managed, it leaves room to expand into a larger disaster where relationships may suffer which causes unnecessary friction in the church. A possible resolution for a pastor who may be afraid of confrontation is to appoint a person who has the gift of administration (Chapter 2) to handle and oversee the execution of all administrative duties of the church. This position is normally referred to as an executive pastor, advisor to the pastor or church administrator. This would allow the pastor to continue to effectively lead the congregation without having to lose face for what could be known as "the necessary evil," which is conflict.[180]

There are some leaders who will not only confront conflict head on but many times they are the one who is guilty of causing the issue. Whichever the case, conflict will remain a part of any work. A leader who is trained to deal with issues can handle various undesirable challenges.

Jesus was not immune to controversy. As a matter of fact, He was surrounded by conflict in many places where He traveled. His opposition was frequently with the Pharisees, the Sadducees and the scribes. It seemed that they followed Him daily in order to trap Him with biblical laws, political issues, and social concerns. On many occasions He was accused of blasphemy, but overcame the disputes by using the word of God, as He understood His authority and from where the opposition was coming (Mt 12). It did not seem that He was welcomed in the synagogue but the synagogue leaders were always somewhere nearby.

---

[180]Ibid., 91.

A leader will always face opposition but one must be prepared and equipped to effectively handle conflict that may sometimes question their authority and stance on issues. Leaders should expect internal conflicts even though many times they supersede the hurt of external conflicts combated. Judas served the purpose as one of the internal saboteurs that Jesus encountered as he proceeded to hand Him over into the hands of man (Mk 14:10). Spence and Exell writes, "The hand that received 'the sop,' that dipped into the same dish with Jesus, received into its hardened palm the miserable pittance-a slave's price. Ah! Even in the presence of the Holy One could he plot and scheme for his delivery. Let us, when we decry the deed, bow our heads lowly, remembering that we share the same frail nature." Jesus handled this final internal sabotage by allowing the betrayal and crucifixion to take place as planned. This shows leaders that they may also have to endure similar opposition by an internal source.[181]

As a new leader of Christians, Paul experienced conflict when he accepted his calling. He preached the Gospel of Jesus Christ in the synagogues but many were confused concerning his allegiance and desired to kill him. However, his followers helped him to avoid death as they lowered him in a basket through an opening in the wall (Acts 9:20-25). His persecution did not stop with the former because he did not abandon his assignment. As he continued to preach the good news of Christ, he was stoned by a crowd and dragged outside the city. ". . . They stoned Paul and dragged him outside the city, thinking he was dead. But after the

---

[181]H.D.M. Spence and Joseph S. Exell, *The Pulpit Commentary*. Peabody, MA: Hendrickson Publishers, 1985, 268.

disciples had gathered around him, he got up and went back into the city." He continued his mission (Acts 14:19-20). Leaders who desire to be effective in the ministry of the Gospel will endure conflicts which may seem unnecessary but will prove to be a valuable part of leadership development and organization.

Interestingly enough Paul dealt with a situation in the Church at Corinth concerning sexual immorality (1 Cor 5:1-13). In his letter to them, Paul shared with them that he received a report concerning a brother in the church who was involved in a sexual relationship with his father's wife (his step-mother). Paul went further and told the congregants that this type of behavior is not even tolerated among those who are considered pagans yet they are prideful concerning the issue but should rather be saddened by this atrocity. The people knew about the relationship but no one neither stepped up to call out the sin nor corrected the brother involved. Paul gave instructions to turn him over to satan and to separate themselves from the offender because of his sin if he refused to repent, as the church has the right to critique those who confess Christ as Lord. What a conflict!

Today, conflict is not much different than in the days of the Bible. There are confrontations in the church that sometimes lead to physical altercations and church splits. Unfortunately, the church has been so interested in how many members it has or how much money it has made at the end of the year that the things of importance (character development) are often left unattended. Too much attention is given to the feelings of individuals and whether or not they have approved lifestyles that the focus of transforming lives for the Kingdom is overlooked.

Let us take a look at the conflict in the Church of Corinth as if it were happening in your church. A brother in your congregation, who confesses Jesus Christ as Lord and Savior, is involved in sexual indecencies with his stepmother. Mostly everyone in the church knows about it, as gossip is stirring up a multiplicity of feelings among the congregants. Some people do not care what he is doing as long as he does not bother their spouses. Many just like to talk about what they know because they have nothing better to do, and only a few are devastated by the issue because he is one who professes Christ. The pastor is the last one to learn about the conflict but is forced to do something about it as it is causing pandemonium in the church. What should he do? If he takes the biblical approach of lovingly chastising the brother and asking him to repent of his sin, least he is expelled from the church until restoration happens, there possibly could be a challenge. In many cases, the people would rebel against the pastor and say he is wrong for "judging" the brother yet he is within his right as the under shepherd of the church to follow this course of action - as sin that is left unaddressed has a way of causing other issues, as a little corruption unattended will breed more corruption (Gal 5:9).

In many cases, leaders do not deal with this type of conflict because it will make some people very upset because it may be their family member who is involved, it may affect the tithes and offerings or worse, the membership may begin to fall off. Regardless of the outcome, this type of conflict should be addressed for the spiritual betterment of the church.

Other times there may be contentions between those in the fellowship because of differences of opinion. Paul dealt with another situation between two women (Euodias & Syntyche) at the Church at Philippi. The actual conflict was not revealed, however, it was important enough that Paul addressed his knowledge of their contention in the beginning of chapter 4 of Philippians. These women were assumed to be leaders in the Church at Philippi (v. 3) as they were fellow labourers with Paul and others. We should note that disagreements among leaders should be squashed as soon as possible to avoid the spread of disunity in the church. In light of this, Paul requested the aid of fellow labourers to encourage the women to resolve their differences by agreeing with one another with the same mind in the Lord.

Many times the assistance of others is solicited to eradicate disagreements between one another. However, in some cases inquiry of the wrong people is petitioned. If we choose to involve other believers in the resolution of disagreements in the church it is necessary to ensure that they also have the mind of Christ and not a divisive spirit to spread rumors or gossip about what is known.

Here is a conflict resolution example: Eloise approached Penelope at church with a bogus concern. Penelope knew that the incident never happened as Eloise had explained but she indulged her anyway. After Eloise finished expressing her apprehensions, Penelope acknowledged the concern but asked Eloise if she would lead them in prayer for a resolution. Because the complaint was not legitimate, Eloise struggled with appropriate words while praying for resolving a situation that did not exist. Although this complaint was quickly squashed, Eloise never approached Penelope anymore. The unfortunate thing is that Eloise only wanted to start an issue and did not really desire reconciliation;

therefore, she began to avoid Penelope and never spoke to her again. The deception of Eloise was discovered.

In modern day church, disagreements can last for years at a time without the hope of compromise. Unfortunately, these disputes are often fueled by the interference of others and have minimum potential of ever receiving the attention that they deserve for an amicable resolution. This does not contribute to Kingdom service as it destroys the witness of the church for unbelievers.

Occasionally, we will find congregants of modern day churches that do not respect their leadership and continuously conjure false accusations against the leader, not necessarily because things are going wrong but because things are simply, not going their way. Whenever there are more parishioners at a church meeting than in Bible study, it speaks volumes of the carnality of the congregants who only attend the meetings; unfortunately, it also reveals their insatiable appetite to nurture discord. Subsequently, there should be a desire to end all disagreements and conflicts in the church, with a resolution of reconciliation.

Chapter 5
Leadership Field Experience

The information in this chapter is based on the results obtained at the culmination of the leadership class project. It lists in detail the methods used to develop the participants over a six-week period. Although this section is explaining the field experience of this project, it is nevertheless relevant to understand the process used to cultivate this material. Let us begin.

The context for this research was Shalom Baptist Church, Newport News, Virginia. The author selected thirteen people to participate in this study of leadership empowerment. They were all chosen at random as their ages ranged from twenty-one to sixty-eight. There were two group categories: current leaders and potential leaders, of which six were current and seven were potential. Each participant was asked to sign a letter of confidentiality before the sessions began. Then the group was instructed of the order that would be followed throughout the six-weeks.

A data triangulation analysis using a qualitative research method for this project was to improve the understanding and to empower current and potential leaders in a local church setting. The analysis was to test a small group of participants and measure the advancement of their understanding which encompassed five sermons, discussions, prayer sessions, reading assignments and a power lunch which focused on the topic of *Equipping Spirit-Led Leaders: Empowering Current and Potential Leaders for Kingdom Service*, with individual subtopics that pointed back to the main topic. On paper, they were placed into two groups: current and potential leaders of which six of the thirteen were positioned in the current leader's category and the remaining seven were enlisted in the potential leader's category unbeknown to any of the group to avoid the skewing of any test outcomes. The facilitator utilized a pre and post-test questionnaire and other assessment tools such as surveys, crossword puzzles, matching games and an interview, which ascertained and gauged the progress of each participant.

Although people have various learning curves, the combination of, teaching and follow-up was most important. More often than not, congregants attend churches regularly on Sunday morning to hear a sermon but many times they leave the service confused about what they have heard. Because of this concern, it was ensured that the participants for the project would have follow-up assignments after the teaching/preaching session was over to re-emphasize the importance of retaining the information taught for later application.

The first, third and fifth sessions were pointed towards how to effectively lead. The participants were taught how Nehemiah effectively led leaders and various people of Israel in a building project through prayer as they were learning how to deal with internal and external conflict. The second and fourth sessions were pointed towards leadership roles in the church. The participants were taught how Nehemiah peacefully submitted to authority with wisdom from God and not of his own strength. The sixth and final session was pointed toward understanding spiritual gifts. The participants were taught how Nehemiah knew the gifts he possessed and activated them as the need required. The seven motivational (operation) gifts listed were: administration, exhortation, giving, mercy, prophecy, service and teaching. This session seemed to be the most rewarding for the participants as some of the participants never understood whom they were created to be until after the assignments were completed.

The participants enjoyed the intimate setting as they felt that it was conducive to learning. Some of them enjoyed the questionnaires after the sermon and some were fascinated by the class dialogues and their ability to correctly add to the quality of the discussions.

It was also discovered that many of the participants wanted to maintain the intimate teaching sessions beyond the six-weeks and desired to continue in the prayer conference calls that were instituted. Some even requested that Church school classes would pattern its outline after the format of the six-week project as they would be more inclined to attend and more apt to learn. They expressed that the teaching would help them become a better leader and helped them to gain the confidence that they needed to be a quality teacher. The overall consensus of the group was that this project should be used as a training template for other current and potential leaders in the church.

On the flip side, it was ascertained that those who were in the current leadership group struggled to retain the information taught more so than those who were in the potential leadership group. This was partially due to the fact that the absentee rate was highest among those who were classified as current leaders. It seemed as though the current leaders category relied more on what they already knew and what they had been taught in the past as their basis. However, some of the participants began to move toward leadership positions in the church with more confidence and decisiveness and was able to recognize quickly those who exhibited a lack of leadership qualities. The leadership training program that addressed organizational leadership skills, improved the overall understanding of the participants as it related to spiritual gifts, leadership roles in the church, and how to effective lead and was validated by a 0.01 positive outcome.

First Week

The author gave the thirteen participants a pre-test which evolved around the topics of emphasis, namely: understanding spiritual gifts, leadership roles in the church and how to effectively lead. This is designed to test the understanding of each person in the previous areas of concentration. The first sermon was given with a topic of *Pray Before Action* (Neh 1:4-11). The purpose was to teach how to effectively lead through prayer. It was taught that all leaders should pray before engaging in any type of activity. A ten-question survey was given to capture the initial reaction to the sermon and to test how much of the sermon was retained.

Five initial reaction questions were given:

(1) How did the sermon make you feel? Empowered, Sad, Happy, Refreshed, Upset, Confused, Not Sure, (You may write another word not listed).

(2) Was the sermon easy to understand? Yes or No.

(3) Could you find yourself in the sermon? Yes or No.

(4) Was the sermon beneficial for your future growth? Yes or No.

(5) What group of people could benefit from this sermon? Leaders, Non-Leaders, Both Leaders and Non-Leaders, No one, Not Sure. Each had options for questions respectively.

(1) Out of the five initial reaction questions, 50 percent answered that they felt refreshed, 41.66 percent answered that they felt empowered and 8.33 percent answered that they felt happy. For questions (2), (3) and (4), 100 percent

answered Yes to all three questions; (5) 91.66 answered Both Leaders and Non-Leaders, 8.33 percent answered Leaders Only.

Five questions specific to the sermon were given:

(6) What was the first thing Nehemiah did after hearing the news about Jerusalem?

(7) What were the two attributes of God that Nehemiah mentioned?

(8) How did Nehemiah ask for God's attention?

(9) How often did Nehemiah cry out to God?

(10) According to Nehemiah, who had sinned against God?

Each question could be answered with one word or several words but had to remain in the confines of the question in order to be accurate. Out of five sermonic questions, 8.33 percent answered all questions correctly, 58.33 percent answered one question incorrectly, 16.66 percent answered two questions incorrectly and 16.66 percent answered three questions incorrectly. The author was quite encouraged that the participants were excited about the teaching sessions.

Next, the participates were given a word matching activity that tested how much of the sermon was retained.

(1) Nehemiah – Prayed and confessed the sins of him and his family.

(2) Jerusalem – Was destroyed and in ruin.

(3) God – Listened to the prayer of His servant.

(4) King – Has the power to grant requests of his subjects. The findings are these: 60 percent answered all questions correctly, 40 percent answered two questions incorrectly.

The author established a prayer conference call on each Thursday morning for the participants from 7:00 a.m. to 7:30 p.m. Each participant was required to attend the prayer call without being reminded but it was optional for them to pray during the call. This call was designed to develop a regular prayer time. Each participant was asked to pick a leader and pray for them. On the first call there was 61.53 percent participation. Of the participants, 12.5 percent were in the current leader's category, 87.5 percent were in the potential leader's category. 12.5 percent of the current leaders prayed while 62.5 percent of the potential leaders prayed on the same call, while 25 percent, which were current leaders, did not pray. The weekly reading assignment was given for the upcoming session (Neh 2:1-8) and the call was ended.

Second Week

The second sermon was *Leaders Submitting to Their Leader* (Neh 2:1-8). The purpose was to teach how to understand the function of leadership roles through submitting to the one who is in authority. It was taught that a submitted leader is an effective leader, as he or she knows how to respect authority. A ten-question survey was given to capture the initial reaction to the sermon and to test how much of the sermon was retained.

Five initial reaction questions were given:

(1) How did the sermon make you feel? Empowered, Sad, Happy, Refreshed, Upset, Confused, Not Sure, (You may write another word not listed).

(2) Was the sermon easy to understand? Yes or No.

(3) Could you find yourself in the sermon? Yes or No.

(4) Was the sermon beneficial for your future growth? Yes or No.

(5) What group of people could benefit from this sermon? Leaders, Non-Leaders, Both Leaders and Non-Leaders, No one, Not Sure. Each had options for questions respectively.

(1) Out of the five initial reaction questions, 30 percent answered that they felt refreshed, 60 percent answered that they felt empowered and 10 percent answered that they felt happy. For questions (2), (3) and (4), 100 percent answered Yes to all three questions, (5) 100 percent answered Both Leaders and Non-Leaders. The participant who answered Leaders Only last week changed their answer to Both Leaders and Non-Leaders in the Second Week.

Five questions specific to the sermon were given:

(1) What were the three main points of the sermon?

(2) According to the sermon, to whom does leaders answer?

(3) The heart of the king is in whose hands?

(4) How did Nehemiah consult God?

(5) Who was ultimately in charge of the decision for Nehemiah?

Each question could be answered with one word or several words but had to remain in the confines of the question in order to be correct. Out of five sermonic questions, 20 percent answered all questions correctly, 10 percent answered one question incorrectly, 50 percent answered two questions incorrectly and 20 percent answered three questions incorrectly. The author adjusted the style of delivery in order to ensure that all were able to understand all present information clearly.

Next, the participants were given a ten-question crossword puzzle that tested how much of the sermon was retained. The questions were:

Across (1) The city that was in ruin – Jerusalem.

(2) Nehemiah prayed for – Israel.

(3) The father of Nehemiah – Hachaliah.

(4) Nehemiah needed mercy from – The King.

(5) Nehemiah did this after hearing the sad news – Wept.

Down (6) Nehemiah began to – Pray.

(7) What did Nehemiah and his forefathers do – Sinned.

(8) God keeps this with them that love Him – Covenant.

(9) What job did Nehemiah have – Cupbearer.

(10) The brother of Nehemiah – Hanani.

The findings are these: 30 percent answered all questions correctly, 30 percent answered one question incorrectly, 20 percent answered two questions incorrectly, 10 percent answered five questions incorrectly, and 10 percent answered six questions incorrectly.

The second prayer conference call was held. Each participant was required to attend the prayer call without being reminded but it was optional for them to pray during the call. On the second call there was 46.15 percent participation. Of the participants, 100 percent were in the potential leader's category. 25 percent of the potential leaders prayed. There were no current leaders on this call. The weekly reading assignment was given for the upcoming session (Neh 3:1-32) and the call was ended.

Third Week

The third sermon was *Internal Conflict* (Neh 3:1-32). The purpose was to teach that leaders should not always despise conflict but face it head on. Conflict can come from inside or outside the church but should be used as a tool of improvement for the leader and for those who follow. A ten-question survey was given to capture the initial reaction to the sermon and to test how much of the sermon was retained.

Five initial reaction questions were given:

(1) How did the sermon make you feel? Empowered, Sad, Happy, Refreshed, Upset, Confused, Not Sure, (You may write another word not listed)

(2) Was the sermon easy to understand? Yes or No

(3) Could you find yourself in the sermon? Yes or No

(4) Was the sermon beneficial for your future growth? Yes or No

(5) What group of people could benefit from this sermon? Leaders, Non-Leaders, Both Leaders and Non-Leaders, No one, Not Sure. Each had options for questions respectively.

(1) Out of the five initial reaction questions, 63.63 percent answered that they felt refreshed, 27.27 percent answered that they felt empowered and 8.33 percent answered that they felt happy. For questions (2), (3) and (4), 100 percent answered Yes to all three questions, (5) 100 percent answered Both Leaders and Non-Leaders.

Five questions specific to the sermon were given:

(1) What was the sermon topic today?

(2) What was being repaired?

(3) Who refused to work under their supervisors?

(4) How many gates were there?

(5) Who was the first group to start the work? Each question could be answered with one word or several words but had to remain in the confines of the question in order to be correct. Out of five sermonic questions, 63.63 percent answered all questions correctly, 18.18 percent answered one question incorrectly and 18.18 percent answered two questions incorrectly. The author was sure that everyone would score 100 percent on this test because of the descriptive delivery.

Next, they were given a Conflict Management Style Activity to determine the conflict style of the individual and how they usually react in a conflicting situation. The conflict styles were avoiding, collaborating, competing, compromising or harmonizing. The avoiding style will elude confrontation at any cost which calms the situation immediately but leaves unresolved concerns. The collaborating style caters to both sides of the issue, which brings the best outcomes but takes a lot of energy to manage. The competing style is dictatorial but is mission oriented and can fester ill will and bad feelings. The compromising style is similar to the collaborating style however with the compromising style all sides are considered equal but rarely does anything change which leaves unhappy people. The harmonizing style breed's healthy relationships but can expose the weaknesses of those who may not be up to par with the desired program.[182]

The findings are these: 63.63 percent were collaborating style, 27.27 percent were compromising style and 9.09 percent were avoiding style. To the surprise of the author, no one claimed the competing or harmonizing style but for the most part everyone was neutral.

---

[182]Conflict Management Style Assessment

The third prayer conference call was held. Each participant was required to attend the prayer call without being reminded but it was optional for them to pray during the call. On the third call there was 53.84 percent participation. Of the participants, 100 percent were in the potential leader's category. 87.5 percent of the potential leaders prayed while 12.5 of the participants did not pray. There were no current leaders on this call. The weekly reading assignment was given for the upcoming session (Neh 3:17-32; 4:7-9) and the call was ended.

Fourth Week

For this week, only a Leadership Style Survey was distributed. The author operated under the premise that participants could experience information overload. To avoid participant burnout, only one survey was given for the week. The purpose was to understand leadership roles by determining the leadership style of the individual and how they handle leading others. The leadership styles were authoritarian, delegative and participative. The authoritarian style leaders are driven, goal oriented and precise in their delivery. This works well when time is a factor but can breed hostility to those who receive directions from the authoritarian as they may be deemed to be bossy, pushy and over the top. The delegative style leaders are less pushy but rely heavy upon the people who work in their down line. This works well when there is time to brainstorm and receive follow-up from the delegated subordinate about the task at hand. However, this style can cause the leader some heartache if the delegated subordinate is not trustworthy or knowledgeable. The participative style leaders regularly solicit ideas and input from a group but ultimately make the final decisions. It is a group motivator.

The findings are these: 7.69 percent were authoritarian style, 7.69 percent were delegative style and 84.61 percent were participative style. To the surprise of the author, the majority was somewhat neutral.[183]

The fourth prayer conference call was held. Each participant was required to attend the prayer call, but it was optional for them to pray during the call. On the fourth call there was 61.53 percent participation. Of the participants, 12.5 percent were in the current leader's category, 87.5 percent were in the potential leader's category. 37.5 percent of the potential leaders prayed, while 62.5 percent, which were current leaders, did not pray. The weekly reading assignment was given for the upcoming session (Neh 6:1-9) and the call was ended.

Fifth Week

The fourth sermon was *Dealing with Duplicitous People* (Neh 6:1-9). The purpose was to teach that leaders should know those who labor among them. This was also a sermon to teach how to effectively lead through conflict resolution. Leaders should seek the Lord in all decisions and be wise in the response to a person who may be in direct contradiction of their leadership. A ten-question survey was given to capture the initial reaction to the sermon and to test how much of the sermon was retained.

Five initial reaction questions were given:
(1) How did the sermon make you feel? Empowered, Sad, Happy, Refreshed,
    Upset, Confused, Not Sure, (You may write another word not listed).
(2) Was the sermon easy to understand? Yes or No.

---

[183]Leadership Style Survey

(3) Could you find yourself in the sermon? Yes or No.

(4) Was the sermon beneficial for your future growth? Yes or No.

(5) What group of people could benefit from this sermon? Leaders, Non-Leaders, Both Leaders and Non-Leaders, No one, Not Sure. Each had options for questions respectively.

(1) Out of the five initial reaction questions, 92.30 percent answered that they felt empowered and 7.69 percent answered that they felt refreshed. For questions (2) 100 percent answered Yes, (3) 92.30 percent answered Yes, 7.69 percent answered Neither Yes or No (4), 92.30 percent answered Yes, 7.69 percent answered Neither Yes or No (5) 92.30 percent answered Both Leaders and Non-Leaders, 7.69 percent answered Leaders Only.

Five questions specific to the sermon were given:

(1) What was the sermon topic today?

(2) What does duplicitous mean? Circle only one number.

(3) What tactic did Sanballat use against Nehemiah to come down to meet with him?

(4) How many times did Sanballat try to get Nehemiah to come down to meet with him?

(5) How far was the place Ono from Jerusalem? Each question could be answered with one word or several words but had to remain in the confines of the question in order to be correct. Out of five sermonic questions, 30.76 percent answered all questions correctly, 53.84 percent answered one question incorrectly and 15.38 percent answered two questions incorrectly. The author was concerned about the way the sermon was delivered as the large majority missed the same one question.

There was a refresher free style questionnaire given to monitor how much information has been retained over the previous weeks. This was not a test, which means no data was collected for reporting, but the questions are as follows:

(1) What was Nehemiah 1-9 about?

(2) Who were the established enemies of Nehemiah?

(3) What did Sanballat want with Nehemiah?

(4) What was Nehemiah doing?

(5) Was Nehemiah successful in his endeavors? Explain.

(6) How did the people react to Nehemiah?

(7) Would you be afraid if you were Nehemiah?

(8) How did Nehemiah handle his opposition?

(9) How would you handle this type of situation?

The fifth prayer conference call was held. Each participant was required to attend the prayer call, without being reminded but it was optional for them to pray during the call. On the fifth call there was 61.53 percent participation. Of the participants, 12.5 percent were in the current leader's category, 87.5 percent were in the potential leader's category. 57.14 percent of the potential leaders prayed while 42.86 percent, which were current leaders, did not pray. The weekly reading assignment was given for the upcoming session (Neh 12:44-47; Eph 4:11; Ro 12:6-8; 1 Cor 12:8-11; Neh 12:26) and the call was ended. The author noticed a pattern among those who were deemed current leaders. The current leaders represented 46.15 percent of the total thirteen participants with only 16.66 percent overall representation on the prayer call.

The author sponsored a power lunch at a local restaurant for the thirteen participants. It was necessary to give the participants a change of scenery and also reward them for their commitment and desire to understand the many facets of leadership. A Spiritual Gifts Analysis was assigned. The purpose was to determine the motivational gifts (Ro 12:6-8) of the individual and why they respond to situations in the manner in which they do. Each leader should be aware of his or her gift(s) to ensure they receive proper placement in the service of ministry.

The spiritual gifts styles were administration, exhortation, giving, mercy, prophecy, service and teaching. The administration gift focuses on organization, details, the ability to delegate and goal accomplishments. The exhortation gift focuses on encouragement and bringing the right words of comfort when needed. The giving gift focuses on the ability to provide financial or necessary resources with gladness for the Lord's work. The mercy gift has compassion for anyone who may suffer physical, emotional and/or spiritual maladies. The prophecy gift focuses on the proclamation of the truth in black and white and can discern the intent of an individual almost immediately. The service gift focuses on meeting the needs of others with great enthusiasm. Finally, the teaching gift focuses on the practical explanation and application of the Scriptures.[184]

The findings are these: 38.46 percent had the administration gift as their primary gift, 7.69 percent had the exhortation gift as their primary gift, 15.38 percent had the giving gift as their primary gift, 23.07 percent had the mercy gift

---

[184]Spiritual Gifts Analysis.

as their primary gift and 15.38 percent had the service gift as their primary gift. The author was amazed that no one registered as having the prophecy gift as their primary, secondary or third gift.

Sixth Week

The fifth and final sermon was *Understanding the Gifts of Self and Others* (Neh 8:9; 12:44-47). The purpose was to teach how knowing and activating the motivational gifts are important to the work of the church. It was taught that all leaders have at least one primary gift and become fulfilled when used. The variety and distinctions of gifts was explained (Eph 4:11, 1 Cor 12:8-11) but the motivational gifts in Romans 12:6-8 were highlighted particularly for this study. A ten-question survey was given to capture the initial reaction to the sermon and to test how much of the sermon was retained.[185]

Five initial reaction questions were given:

(1) How did the sermon make you feel? Empowered, Sad, Happy, Refreshed, Upset, Confused, Not Sure, (You may write another word not listed).

(2) Was the sermon easy to understand? Yes or No.

(3) Could you find yourself in the sermon? Yes or No.

(4) Was the sermon beneficial for your future growth? Yes or No.

(5) What group of people could benefit from this sermon? Leaders, Non-Leaders, Both Leaders and Non-Leaders, No one, Not Sure. Each had options for questions respectively.

---

[185]Fortune, *Discover Your God-Given Gifts*... 15.

(1) Out of the five initial reaction questions, 27.27 percent answered that they felt refreshed, 63.63 percent answered that they felt empowered and 9.09 percent answered that they felt happy. For questions (2) 100 percent answered Yes, (3) 90.90 percent answered Yes, 9.09 percent answered Neither Yes or No (4), 100 percent answered Yes, (5) 100 percent answered Both Leaders and Non-Leaders.

Five questions specific to the sermon was given:

(6) Everyone has at least one motivational gift?

(7) What are the 3 different name categories of gifts mentioned? Circle one number.

(8) List 2 out of 4 of Nehemiah's motivational gifts that were mentioned? Circle one number.

(9) Have you discovered what the top three of your motivational gifts are?

(10) What are the top three of your motivational gifts from the spiritual gifts analysis? Each question could be answered with one word or several words but had to remain in the confines of the question in order to be correct. Out of five sermonic questions, 63.63 percent answered all questions correctly, 27.27 percent answered one question incorrectly, 9.09 percent three questions incorrectly.

The author was so appreciative of the contribution by the thirteen participants that a commencement ceremony was held immediately after all test papers were turned in for analysis. Each participant received a certificate for completion of *Equipping Spirit-Led Leaders: Empowering Current and Potential Leaders for Kingdom Service*.

Exit Interviews were given to each person after the class was over. There were ten questions asked of each participant, respectively:

(1) Can you remember the sermon that had the most impact on you to date?

(2) How has it helped you?

(3) Did you feel this style of preaching/teaching was effective for your learning?

(4) Had you read and understood the book of Nehemiah before this project?

(5) Could you effectively discuss the book of Nehemiah if you were engaged in a conversation tomorrow?

(6) What was the most operative tool used for you to retain more info?

(7) Do you better understand spiritual gifts, leadership roles in the church and how to effectively lead?

(8) Do you have any final comments?

The questions are answered below respectively:

(1) Understanding spiritual gifts was the most popular lesson as each participant was excited to know why they respond to situations the way they do.

(2) Now they know that it is because of the gifts that they possess. One participant expressed how he wants to use his gifts to assist the pastor in the many tasks that he must do.

(3) They felt that the intimate setting was conducive to learning and the surveys were effective for retaining information. One of the participants felt if Church school was taught with the methods used in this project that they would attend regularly.

(4) About 50 percent of the participants had read Nehemiah but was not completely clear on the subject matter but now the context of the Scripture is understandable.

(5) All of the participants felt that they could converse about Nehemiah. One participant stated that she had already started discussions about what she learned.

(6) 100 percent of the class stated that the teaching was the most effective tool for them to learn however, they raved about the surveys at the ending of each sermon as it helped with loose ends.

(7) 100 percent of the participants believe that their understanding has improved over the six-week timeframe.

(8) Some of the final comments were they wanted to explore more information concerning their gifts and wanted to begin using them for Kingdom service. They shared that this project has helped them to become better leaders and teachers. One participant admired the teacher, as she feels empowered and inspired to serve. 23.07 percent of the participants wanted to continue the prayer conference call and 50 percent of the class states that their confidence level received a boost by hearing how Nehemiah handled various situations. Finally, 100 percent of the participants expressed the appreciation for being included in the project.

    The author gave the thirteen participants a post-test, which evolved around the topics of emphasis namely: understanding spiritual gifts, leadership roles in the church and how to effectively lead. It was the same test that was given at the inception of the class as the pre-test. This was designed to test whether or not the understanding of each person has improved in the previous areas of concentration. The study verified that after the training program there was a 0.01 percent variance in what the thirteen participants had learned. The hypothesis was validated.

Chapter 6

Learning of Recommended Readings

It is critical to provide a large scope of references that will demonstrate balanced research on the subject matter of leadership. While investigating the challenges that persists as current and potential leaders are trained to improve their leadership understanding, it has been discovered that authors share various views of what is considered ineffective leadership in the Christian Church. The collection of sources provided range from academic writings to devotional works that will serve as a guide for leadership growth. We will explore various selections of literature regarding spiritual gifts; leadership roles in the church, and how to effectively lead in order to efficiently convey the message through a consolidation of biblical, historical and theological sources.

Biblical Assessment

These are the following biblically based books that largely contributed to this work. This list is not exhaustive; however, these authors provided the necessary validity for the biblical support of this leadership paradigm.

In the book, *Cultivating The Discipline Of Prayer: The Key To Having Power With God*, Dr. Geoffrey V. Guns writes an impressive study guide identifying the impact that prayer has on the life of people who are willing to embark upon this endeavor. It defines prayer as a secret weapon that will foil the plan of the opposition if put into practice. He discusses the importance of prayer in the life of the believer, as it is an act of communion and relationship.

The book, *The Art Of Prayer: A Simple Guide To Conversation With God*, by Timothy Jones, is a fascinating work that gives a simple guideline to prayer:

how to approach God, how to speak to God and how to continue pressing beyond self. It explains that individuals have a desire to communicate with God, even if there is not a belief that God will answer. It is a remarkable guide, offering insights into petitioning God, as well as anticipating His expected response.

In the book, *A Silent Path to God* by James E. Griffiss, the author speaks to the inner being of an individual as it relates to prayer. Griffiss shows that one cannot pray without God being involved in the two-way communication.

The book, *Life with God: Reading the Bible for Spiritual Transformation* by Richard J. Foster, deals with the idea of spending time with God, and the productive nature that it induces. This offering identifies the necessity of relationships and the transformative process that begins by centering our lives on God and on those disciplines that God desires of His people. It is designed to encourage spiritual transformation after an introspective analysis has been conducted. This writing is an internal map that will lead to a life of wholeness.

The sermon, *The Skills of Leadership*, *Part 3* by Dr. William D. Tyree, III, addresses leadership roles in the church. It conveys the message that it is ultimately the responsibility of the leader to invest in each person under his or her leadership. It suggests that leaders are to be aware of the strengths and weaknesses of the team and bring balance where there is imbalance among the group.

The Pulpit Commentary, by H. D. M. Spence and Joseph S. Exell, expounds upon a complete exegetical breakdown of historical, theological, and biblical foundations that answers questions in various settings. It is a clear and concise contemporary explanation of the Scriptures that is filled with a multiplicity of verse-by-verse exposition. This commentary is loaded with an incorporation of facts, truths, and historical information.

Transformational Coaching by Dr. Joseph Umidi, provides a platform for coaching and cutting edge counseling in order to connect the missing pieces of ministry. It deals with emotional and spiritual transformational dimensions of the innermost being on various levels. It is a work that can transcend into the marketplace for successful impact.

In *Biblical Interpretation: A Roadmap* by Frederick C. Tiffany and Sharon H. Ringe, the authors give guidelines as to how to extract specific information from the biblical text with accuracy. It helps one discover the right questions to ask in order to arrive at a sound interpretation of the text.

Leadership Secrets from the Bible by Lorin Woolfe compares the patriarchs of old to the business managers of today with biblical references. It highlights the successes and failures experienced. This book was helpful to identify leadership roles in the church and how to effectively lead the masses from voluminous perspectives.

The Leader Within by Michael Thomas Scott addresses the resurrection of the leader within. It encourages self-development through biblical principles and provides the insight for ministry on any level. This book causes a potential leader to introspectively perceive themselves as a leader with dominion as God intended. It also provides a current leader the motivation for self-improvement.

Historical Assessment

These are the following historical books that largely contributed to this work. This list is not exhaustive; however, these authors provided the necessary validity for the historical support of the leadership paradigm.

Josephus: The Essential Writings by Paul L. Maier discusses a historical view of Jewish Antiquities and the Jewish War. It discourses a chronological account of the Jews and the transitions endured in ancient times.

The commentary *Ezra, Nehemiah, Esther* by Mark Roberts and Lloyd J. Ogilvie, gives a historical approach of the way in which Nehemiah successfully led the people of Israel in the rebuilding of the city walls. He was able to identify leaders and delegate authority to those who could be held accountable for the way in which they led.

The Substance of Things Hoped For: A Memoir of African-American Faith, by Samuel DeWitt Proctor, is a book that expounds on the memory of African-American faith and the legacy that has been left to carry on. It is a historical backdrop of what church meant to a specific group of people and still rings true in many current arenas.

The Mentor Leader by Tony Dungy with Nathan Whitaker discusses the consistent development of winning teams of people by mentoring potential leaders through leadership. It provides various facets of leadership, which produces a team atmosphere that encourages reaching out to help those who are in your corner. This is a superb resource to develop, build and positively influence teams of people that will make the maximum impact.

Josephus And The Jews by F. J. Foakes Jackson, is a theological and historical approach of the early church and its functionality according to Josephus, the historian.

A Passion For Faithfulness: Wisdom From The Book Of Nehemiah by J. I. Packer addresses Nehemiah's passion to manage and coordinate for the good of the organization. However, one cannot only count on processes and procedures to accomplish the task but rather trust God for direction, growth and blessings.

The Leaders Companion: Insights on Leadership through the Ages by J. T. Wren, gives an historical overview of the various faces of leadership with examples from a wide variety of authors. The different aspects of demonstrated thought and theory are timeless from Plato and Aristotle to Richard M. Nixon. These viable perspectives help to support the definition of how to effectively lead.

Prayers Ancient and Modern, by Mary Wilder Tileston gives a riveting collection of short heart-felt prayers for various occasions. This book provided a historical snapshot of the prayer-disciplined lives of profound authors and Early Church Fathers.

The Soul of Leadership by Deepak Chopra, alludes to the fact that self-motivation plays a large part in the life of an individual. It is a transformational piece that will unlock the secrets to leadership, and the steps to achieve the potential for greatness because of what lies within the soul of the individual. The perceptive theme of the book is that each person holds the key to his or her joys, sorrows, successes and failures. Anyone can become a great leader.

Dealing with Difficult People: How to Deal with Nasty Customers, Demanding Bosses and Annoying Co-workers by Roberta Cava discusses several techniques to deal with rude, unhappy, divisive, and duplicitous people in a way that is a win-win situation for all. It shares how-to methods of handling conflict and stressful situations with flair and professionalism. This was an extremely good contemporary read as multiple techniques were given to diffuse real life situations.

The Last of The Giants: Lifting The Veil On Islam And The End Times by George Otis Jr., is a historical and in-depth outlook on the movement of Islam and the way in which Western Christianity can intercede in the spirit realm on their behalf.

Theological Assessment

These are the following theological books that largely contributed to this work. This list is not exhaustive; however, these authors provided the necessary validity for the theological support of the leadership paradigm.

The Gift of Prophecy in the New Testament and Today by Wayne Grudem takes a theological glance at the sign gifts. He takes a radical approach in the explanation of canonical authority as it relates to Old Testament and New Testament prophecies, which caused critical analyses. This book was a necessary read and applicable for anyone who would consider teaching on spiritual gifts.

I Believe in the Holy Spirit by Michael Green discusses the person of the Holy Spirit and the many facets of gifts. He contends that many in the Christian Church know very little about the Holy Spirit and even less about the gifts that accompany the relationship. Although Green has not activated any of these gifts personally, he tactfully exposes the Scriptures that will illuminate the need to understand spiritual gifts.

Warren Bennis and Patricia Ward Biederman, wrote *Organizing Genius: The Secret of Creative Collaboration,* showed how working together is the order of the day, and that it is impractical to work alone when strength can be found in assistance. It gives ways of collaborating with others to arrive at a goal perhaps not met if approached alone. It encourages creative thinking and new ways of achieving a positive end result.

In Jason E. Vickers book, *Minding the Good Ground: A Theology for Church Renewal,* he discusses the "The Nature of the Church" - the theology of the church, and how it can be renewed through the power of the Spirit of God. It defines the mission of the Church and how it exists.

In *Introductory Lectures in Systematic Theology,* Henry C. Thiessen lectures on various aspects of God and practically conveys theological truths with Scriptural support. This work encompasses the nature and works of the Triune God. This book was a robust thought toward leaders for effective ministry.

Systematic Theology: An Introduction to Biblical Doctrine by Wayne Grudem, is an introduction to biblical doctrine and is written for those who want a closer look at biblical doctrine in a more contemporary fashion. Each chapter is broken into bite size categories with specific scriptural foundations for a closer look at the theology of the Church.

The Power of Prayer in a Believer's Life by Charles Spurgeon addresses several ways to achieve the outcome of prayer. It dispels the mysteries of prayer for every situation in a way that it illuminates the correct pathway. This book was an impactful resource for prayer posture and praying the Scriptures for faith-filled results.

Christian Theology by Millard J. Erickson discusses the Triune God and lays out the disciplined foundation for the Christian Church. This study guide identified the factors that are critical to the belief of a Christian, which shapes thoughts and ideas, which can be controversial in nature. Although this material can be historical and theological, it still shows how important God is in every aspect of the life of a Christian through relationship and knowing the Creator.

Introduction to Theology, by Thomas C. Owen and Ellen K. Wondra, is an introduction to systematic theology from the view point of Anglican Episcopal perspectives. It gives a contemporary and historical discussion, which is based on scriptural foundations.

Essentials of Evangelical Theology by Donald Bloesch is an evangelical work that brings a challenge to what a person believes. It gives a balance to traditional thought versus contemporary ideas as biblical and historical theory is dissected. This work adds flavor to even the more pristine avenues of thought.

Let Us Pray by Terry Thomas gives a vivacious account of what it means to have a disciplined prayer life, as a prayerless life is considered a defeated life. Prayer is defined as a gift from God for the body of Christ and designed to bring one closer to God through this familiar line of communication. This book gives an extensive theological and biblical perspective on a larger scale.

Chapter 7

Leadership Research of General Reflections

This book began as a project for dissertation purposes but soon developed into a basic guide to instruct and empower small groups, individuals, churches and organizations in the methods of how to induce quality leadership in the church. It is based on research of African American churches located in an urban downtown area which is overrun with drugs, prostitution and a plethora of criminal behavior. Many people are afraid to visit the area because of the reputation that it holds which sometimes makes it difficult to attract non-community residents. However, it is realized that the Church is assigned to the community to bring hope to an otherwise devastating situation. This premise suggests that the Church should be in biblical order to be able to influence the community, its surrounding regions and the uttermost parts of the world. Therefore, the passion to train leaders in the Church to be effective in any capacity in which they serve is necessary in order to maximize impact on the communal environment.

Therefore, this draws attention to a more distressing theme; the lack of effective leadership in the church. Too often people in our churches adhere to non-biblical policies of their church but know very little of anything about what the Scriptures state concerning Godly-leadership in general. It is believed that if the latter is addressed, then the former will be the exception not the rule…thus the birth of *Equipping Spirit-Led Leaders.*

It was observed that many who serve in a leadership capacity rarely understand what to do in the leadership role in which they hold. Consequently, the people of the church are sometimes placed in positions that they are not qualified to handle and lack effectiveness. This causes a trickle-down gross deficiency to those who serve in the down line of the assumed leader. It is suggested that there is a much needed shift from leadership mediocrity to quality leadership in our churches. The current leadership needs to be trained and the potential leaders need to be empowered in the context by understanding spiritual gifts, leadership roles in the church and how to effectively lead. It is to this end that this work established a paradigm to enable those in the context to be adequately educated and empowered for Kingdom service.

This project is also designed for replication perhaps with slight modifications if any other entity has a desire to shift from leadership mediocrity to quality leadership in their church. It is understood that "Rome was not built in a day" nor will the improvement of an entire congregation's understanding transform overnight. It is expected that the percentage of those who grasp the leadership concept will share their empowerment and enthusiasm with others by *Equipping Spirit-Led Leaders*.

BIBLIOGRAPHY

Adam Clarke. *Commentary on Jeremiah 3:15. The Adam Clarke Commentary.* http://www.studylight.org/commentaries/acc/view.cgi?bk=jer&ch=3. 1832.

Adsit, Christopher B. *Personal Disciplemaking: A Step-by-step Guide for Leading a Christian from New Birth to Maturity.* Orlando, FL: Here's Life Publishers, 1996.

Autocratic Leadership http://www.vectorstudy.com/management_topics/autocratic_leadership.htm. (accessed on April 28, 2012).

Bible.org/question/will. (accessed on April 28, 2012).

Bennis, Warren. *The Leadership Advantage: Leader to Leader.* New York, NY: Spring, 1999.

_____. *Organizing Genius: The Secret of Creative Collaboration.* New York, NY: Basic Books, A member of the Perseus Books Group, 1997.

Blanchard, Ken. *Leadership and the One Minute Manager: Increasing Effectiveness Through Situational Leadership.* New York, NY: Blanchard Management Corporation, 1985.

Block, P. *Stewardship: Choosing Service Over Self-Interest.* San Francisco, CA: Berrett-Koehler Publishers, 1993.

Bloesch, Donald. *Essentials of Evangelical Theology.* 2 vols. New York, NY: Harper and Row, 1978.

Bounds, E. M. *The Weapon of Prayer.* Grand Rapids, MI: Baker Book House, 1975.

Brehon, Barbara A. F. *Reach Me with SMILES.* Lithonia, GA: Publishing by Orman Press, Inc., 2005.

Busenitz, Nathan. *Throwing Prophecy under the* Agabus, (The Cripplegate, March 15, 2012).

Buswell, James Oliver. *A Systematic Theology of the Christian Religion.* 2 volumes in 1. Grand Rapids: Zondervan Publishing House, 1963.

Cava, Robert. *Dealing with Difficult People: How to Deal with Nasty Customers, Demanding Bosses and Annoying Co-workers*. Buffalo, NY: Firefly Books Inc., 2004.

Caldwell, C., Bischoff, S. J., & Karri, R. *The Four Umpires: A Paradigm for Ethical Leadership.* Smithfield, RI: Journal of Business Ethics, 2002.

Carm.org/junia-apostle.

Christian Mentoring Leadership. HYPERLINK "http://christianmentoringandleadership.com/2011/07/06/a-theology-of-christian-leadership-in-the-beginning-create" http://christianmentoringandleadership.com/2011/07/06/a-theology-of-christian-leadership-in-the-beginning-create. (accessed on April 28, 2012).

Chopra, Deepak. *The Soul of Leadership.* New York, NY: Harmony Books, 2010.

Clawson, J. G. *Level Three Leadership: Getting Below the Surface.* Upper Saddle River, NJ: Prentice-Hall, Inc., 1999.

Conner, W. T. *Christian Doctrine*, Nashville, TN: Broadman Press, 1937.

Cullmann, Oscar. *Jesus and the Revolutionaries.* Harper & Row Publishers, New York, Evanston, and London, 1970.

Democratic Leadership. http://www.vectorstudy.com/management_ topics /democratic_leadership.htm. (accessed on April 28, 2012).

Drane, John. *Introducing the New Testament.* New York, NY: Harper & Row Publishers, 1986.

Driscoll, Mark. *On Church Leadership.* Crossway Books, 2008.

Dungy, Tony with Nathan Whitaker. *The Mentor Leader.* Carol Stream, IL: Tyndale House Publishers, Inc., 2010.

Eims, Leroy. *Be the Leader You Were Meant to Be: Biblical Principles of Leadership.* Wheaton, IL: Victor Books, 1977.

Elbert, Paul. *Calvin and the Spiritual Gifts* (JETS 22/3 September 1979).

Erickson, Millard J. *Christian Theology.* 1 vol. edition. Grand Rapids: Baker Book House, 1985.

Ferguson, Everett. *Church History: From Christ to Pre-Reformation.* 1 Volume. Grand Rapids, MI: Zondervan, 2005.

Fortune, Don and Kate. *Discover Your God-Given Gifts.* Grand Rapids, MI: Chosen Books, a division of Baker Book House Company, 1987.

Foster, Richard J. *Life With God: Reading the Bible for Spiritual Transformation.* New York, NY: HarperCollins Publishers, 2008.

Foullah, Leopold. *The Characteristics of Good Leadership.* Article published June 2008.

George, Joyce. *The Church.* The Catholic Encyclopedia. Vol. 3. New York, NY: Robert Appleton Company, 1908, 30 Apr. 2012 http://www.newadvent.org/cathen/03744a.htm.

Gibson, James L., John M. Ivancevich, James H. Donnelly, Jr. *Organizations: Behavior, Structure, Processes.* Illinois, Boston, Massachusetts, Sydney, Australia, Irwin, Burr Ridge, 8th ed.

Gonzalez, Justo L. *The Story of Christianity: The Early Church to the Dawn of the Reformation.* New York, NY: HarperCollins Publishers, 2010.

Green, Michael. *I Believe in the Holy Spirit.* Grand Rapids: Wm. B. Eerdmans Publishing Co., 1975.

Griffiss, James E. *A Silent Path to God.*, Philadelphia, PA: Fortress Press, 1980.

Grudem, Wayne. *Systematic Theology: An Introduction to Biblical Doctrine.* Grand Rapids, MI: Zondervan Publishing House, 1994.

_____. *The Gift of Prophecy in the New Testament and Today.* Westchester, IL: Crossway Books, 1988.

Guder, Darrell L. *Missional Church: A Vision for the Sending of the Church in North America.* Grand Rapids, MI: William B. Eerdmans Publishing Company, 1998.

Guns, Geoffrey V. *Cultivating the Discipline of Prayer: The Key to Having Power with God.* Virginia Beach, VA: 2005.

_____. *Setting the House in Order: A Guide for Leading Change in the Local Church.* Virginia Beach, VA: Bright Hope Publishing Company, 2004.

_____. *Spiritual Leadership: A Guide to Developing Spiritual Leaders in the Church.* Lithonia, GA: Orman Press, Inc., 2000.

_____. *The First Essential for Leadership: Faith.* (Sermon preached at 2nd Calvary Baptist Church in Norfolk on 7 January 1996).

Hagin, Kenneth. *The Ministry Gifts.* Fourth Edition, Broken Arrow, OK, RHEMA Bible Training Center, 1992.

Hammett, Edward H. *Spiritual Leadership in a Secular Age: Building Bridges Instead of Barriers*. St. Louis, MO: Chalice Press, 2005.

Harrington, Daniel J. *Who is Jesus? Why is He Important?* Franklin, WI: Sheed & Ward, 1999.

Hinson, Glen. *The Significance of Glossolalia in the History of Christianity.*

Holiness. http://bible.org/seriespage/holiness-god. (accessed February 25, 2012).

Holiness. http://www.thefreedictionary.com/holiness. (accessed February 25, 2012).

Holiness. http://www.sounddoctrine.net/Nick/Holiness_God.htm. (accessed February 25, 2012).

House, Paul R. *Old Testament Theology.* Downers Grove, IL: InterVarsity Press, 1998.

Jackson, F. J. Foakes D.D. *JOSEPHUS AND THE JEWS.* New York, NY: Richard R. Smith, Inc., 1930.

Jesus is fully human. http://www.desiringgod.org/blog/posts/jesus-is-fully-human. (accessed February 25, 2012).

Jesus supernatural. http://www.jesuscentral.com/ji/life-of-jesus-ancient/. (accessed February 25, 2012).

Jones, Timothy. *The Art of Prayer, a Simple Guide to Conversation with God.* Colorado Springs, CO: WaterBrook Press, 2005.

Joyce, George. *The Church*. The Catholic Encyclopedia. Vol. 3. New York: Robert Appleton Company, 1908, 30 Apr. 2012 http://www.newadvent.org/cathen/03744a.htm.

Kostenberger, Andreas. *Biblical Foundations, Women Deacons,* April 24, 2006 in Blog.

Kouzes, James M. and Barry Z. Posner. *Christian Reflections on the Leadership Challenge.* San Francisco, CA: Jossey-Bass, 2006.

_____.*The Leadership Challenge.* San Francisco, CA: Jossey-Bass, 2007. *Laissez-faire Leadership.* http://www.vectorstudy.com /management_ topics/laissez- faire_leadership.htm. (accessed on April 28, 2012).

Lasor, William Sanford, David Allan Hubbard, and Frederic William Bush. *Old Testament Survey.* Grand Rapids, MI/Cambridge, U.K.: William B. Eerdmans Publishing Company, 2nd ed., 1996.

Leader. http://www.nwlink.com/~donclark/leader/leadstl.html. (accessed on April 26, 2012).

Leadership History. http://www.leadershiphistory.com. (accessed on April 26, 2012).

Learn Pray. http://www.ucc.org/assets/pdfs/606LearnPray.pdf. (accessed on April 29, 2012).

Leech, Kenneth. *True Prayer: An Invitation to Christian Spirituality.* San Francisco, CA: Harper and Row Publishers, 1980.

Love. http://www.thefreedictionary.com/love. (accessed February 25, 2012).

Lunceford, Joe E. *Women Likewise: A Closer Look at 1 Timothy 3:11,* Religion Department Georgetown College, March 2011.

Bibleinterp.com/opeds/womlik358015.shtml. (accessed on April 28, 2012).

MacDonald, William. *Believer's Bible Commentary.*

Maier, Paul L. *Josephus: The Essential Writings.* Grand Rapids, MI: Kregel Publications, 1988.

Malphurs, Aubrey and William F. Mancini. *Building Leaders: Blueprints for Developing Leadership at Every Level of Your Church.* Grand Rapids, MI, Published by Baker Books, 2004.

Martin Luther. http://www.who2.com/bio/martin-luther. (accessed on April 27, 2012).

Marshall, Tom. *Understanding Leadership.* Grand Rapids, MI: Baker Books, 2003.

Maxwell, John C. *Developing the Leaders Around You.* Nashville, TN: INVOY, Inc., 1995.

_____.*The 21 Irrefutable Laws of Leadership.* Nashville, TN: Thomas Nelson, 2002.

_____. *The Maxwell Leadership Bible.* Nashville, TN: Thomas Nelson, 2002.

Merkle, Benjamin L. *Why Elders? A Biblical and Practical Guide for Church Members.* Grand Rapids, MI: Published by Kregel Publications, 2009.

Miller, Calvin. *The Empowered Leader: 10 Keys to Servant Leadership.* Nashville, TN: Broadman & Holman Publishers, 1995.

Miller, Herb. *Leadership is the Key: Unlocking Your Ministry Effectiveness.* Nashville, TN: Abingdon Press, 1997.

Millman, Joel. *Ghetto Blasters.* (Forbes Magazine, February 12, 1996).

Mims, Gene. *The Kingdom-Focused Church.* Nashville, TN: Broadman & Holman Publishers, 2003.

Miracles. http://www.jesuschristsavior.net/Miracles.html. (accessed February 25, 2012).

Miraculous Gifts in the Early Church http://www.academia.edu/458797/ Miraculous_Gifts_in_the_Early_Church_A_Historical_Analysis. (accessed on April 28, 2012).

Morgan, G. *Images of Organizations.* Thousand Oaks, CA: Sage Publications, 1997.

nwlink.com/~donclark/leader/leadstl.html. (accessed on January 15, 2015).

Organizational Leadership. http://www.ehow.com/about_6567493_organizational-leadership-definition.html, (accessed February 12, 2012).

Otis, George Jr., *The Last of the Giants: Lifting the Veil on Islam and the End Times* .Grand Rapids, MI: Chosen, 1991.

Packer, J. I. *A Passion for Faithfulness: Wisdom from the Book of Nehemiah.* Wheaton, IL: Crossway Books, 1995.

Passion. http://dictionary.reference.com/browse/passion (accessed October 31, 2011).

Person Christ. http://bible.org/seriespage/person-christ. (accessed February 20, 2012).

Pierce, Gregory E. Augustine. *Activism That Makes Sense: Congregations and Community Organizations.* Chicago, IL: ACTA Publications, 1984.

Pink, Arthur W. *The Ability of God: Prayers of the Apostle Paul.* Chicago, IL: The Moody Bible Institute of Chicago, 1967, 2000.

Proctor, Samuel DeWitt. *The Substance of Things Hoped For: A Memoir of African-American Faith.* Valley Forge, PA: Judson Press, 1999.

Richardson, Cyril. *Early Christian Fathers* (Touchstone 1996).

Righteousness. http://www.biblicalstudies.com/bstudy/theopropr/right.htm. (accessed February 20, 2012).

Roberts, Mark and Lloyd J. Ogilvie. vol. 11, *Ezra, Nehemiah, Esther*, The Preacher's Commentary Series Nashville, TN: Thomas Nelson Inc., 1993.

Sanders, J. Oswald. *Spiritual Leadership.* Revised Edition, Chicago, IL: Moody Bible Institute, 1980.

Scott, Michael Thomas. *The Leader Within*. Temperanceville, VA: Rhema Word Publishing, 2005.

Self-determination. http://www.thefreedictionary.com/self-determination. (accessed February 24, 2012).

Shalom Baptist Church. *CONSTITUTION and By-Laws, Newport News, Virginia:* 1995.

Sofield, Loughlan and Donald H. Kuhn. *The Collaborative Leader: Listening to the Wisdom of God's People.* Notre Dame, IN: 1985.

Spence, H. D. M. and Joseph S. Exell, *The Pulpit Commentary*. Peabody, MA: Hendrickson Publishers, 1985.

Strong, James. *Strong's Exhaustive Concordance*

The Arbinger Institute. *Leadership and Self-Deception: Getting Out of the Box.* San Francisco, CA: Berrett-Koehler Publishers, Inc., 2010.

Thiessen, Henry C. *Introductory Lectures in Systematic Theology.* Grand Rapids, MI: Wm. B. Eerdmans, 1949.

Thomas, Owen C. and Ellen K. Wondra. *Introduction to Theology.* Harrisburg, PA: Morehouse Publishing, 2002.

Thomas, Terry. *An Exploration into the Task of Leadership.* (lecture notes from cluster group/Handout).

_____. *Becoming a Fruit-Bearing Disciple.* Raleigh, NC: Voice of Rehoboth, 2005.

_____. *Let Us Pray*, Raleigh, NC: Voice of Rehoboth, 2005.

Tidwell, Charles A. *Church Administration: Effective Leadership for Ministry.* Nashville, TN: Broadman & Holman Press, 1985.

Tiffany, Frederick C. and Sharon H. Ringe. *Biblical Interpretation: A Roadmap.* Nashville, TN: Abington Press, 1996.

Tileston, Mary Wilder. *Prayers Ancient and Modern.* Printed in the United States of America Arrangement with Little, Brown, and Company, 1928.

Tyree, William D. *The Skills of Leadership, Part 3.* (Sermon preached at 1st Baptist Church Berkley in Norfolk on 25 October 2005).

ucc.org/assets/pdfs/606LearnPray.pdf. (accessed on January 15, 2015).

Umidi, Joseph Dr. *Transformative Coaching: Bridge Building that Impacts, Connects, and Advances the Ministry and the Marketplace.* Maitland, Florida: Xulon Press, 2005.

vectorstudy.com/management_topics/autocratic_leadership.htm. (accessed on April 28, 2012).

Vine, W. E., Merrill F. Unger, William White, Jr. *Vines Complete Expository Dictionary*, 1996.

Weems, Jr., Lovett H. *Church Leadership: Vision, Team, Culture, and Integrity.* Nashville, TN: Abingdon Press 1993.

Wernerbiblecommentary.org/?q=book/print/391. (accessed on January 15, 2015).

Woolfe, Lorin W. *Leadership Secrets from the Bible.* New York, NY: Published by MJF Books, 2002.

Whitcomb, John C. *Nehemiah, in The Wycliffe Bible Commentary*

White, John. *Excellence in Leadership: the Pattern of Nehemiah.* Downers Grove, IL: Intervarsity Press, 1986.

Wren, J. T. *The Leaders Companion: Insights on Leadership through the Ages.* New York, NY: The Free Press, 1995.

APPENDIX A
Leadership Survey For Pastors

One of the newer chapters that I added to the manuscript was a five question leadership survey which was given to pastors from various denominations. The questions were:

1. What is the most critical issue that you notice with the majority of your servant leaders?
2. How long does it take for you to place those who migrate from other ministries into leadership positions after training, how long for those who are already in house?
3. Please name at least three criteria that are necessary before placing servant leaders into leadership positions.
4. On a 0-100% scale, what percentage do you trust your current leadership staff?
5. Have you ever had to remove a volunteer servant leader from position, if so, what was the reason?

They were also asked to send a copy of their organizational chart so it can be published under the sample organizational charts section in the book as examples for those who may need a template after which to pattern.

When the question about the most critical issue in their leadership was asked, 4 out of 5 pastors responded that they have the most issues with leaders being committed (accountable) to the service of ministry. When asked how long it takes for servant leaders who migrate from other churches and other denominations 4 out of 5 pastors responded that all servant leaders who migrate must go through a six months to a year training process in order to serve as a leader in their ministry.

The pastor who was the fifth responder stated that he does not allow lay leaders (deacons or trustees) to serve in leadership positions if they migrate from another ministry. They felt that lay leaders who leave one ministry may bring something unpleasant with them when they arrive at the receiving ministry. When asked what were the three criteria that are necessary before leaders are placed in position 5 out of 5 responses were stewardship, commitment and integrity. When asked on a 0-100% scale, what percentage did they trust their current leadership staff 4 out of 5 pastors said they trust their servant leaders about 90% with the task in which they have been given. There was only one pastor who stated, "I have 100% trust that they will operate with integrity. I also have 100% knowledge that everyone has blind spots. Therefore, we have very clear and specific accountability structures in place for every leader (including myself)." This leadership may take some time to create an environment that fosters this type of relationship. When asked have they ever had to remove a volunteer servant leader from position, if so, what was the reason, 3 out of 5 said yes and the reasons were for nonproductive outcomes and the lack of commitment.

The final item requested from the pastors was the organizational chart in which they used for their ministry hierarchy and if they had revised it from an original. Only a few charts were received thus it was necessary to develop our own. It had been discovered that many churches do not have a functional organizational chart but utilize a more traditional approach of all leaders reporting to the senior pastor. They basically have an unwritten plan that was adopted 100 years ago which often causes a misunderstanding in the hierarchy of authority.

APPENDIX B
Sample Organizational Charts

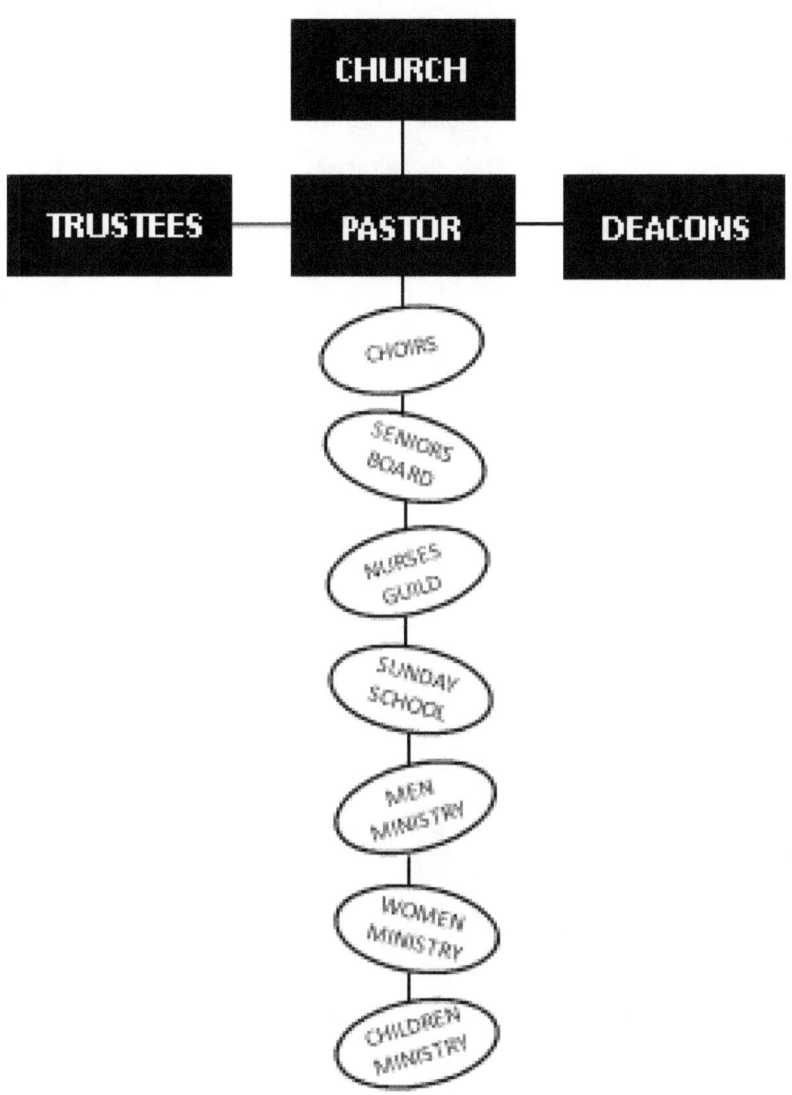

Sample Organizational Chart

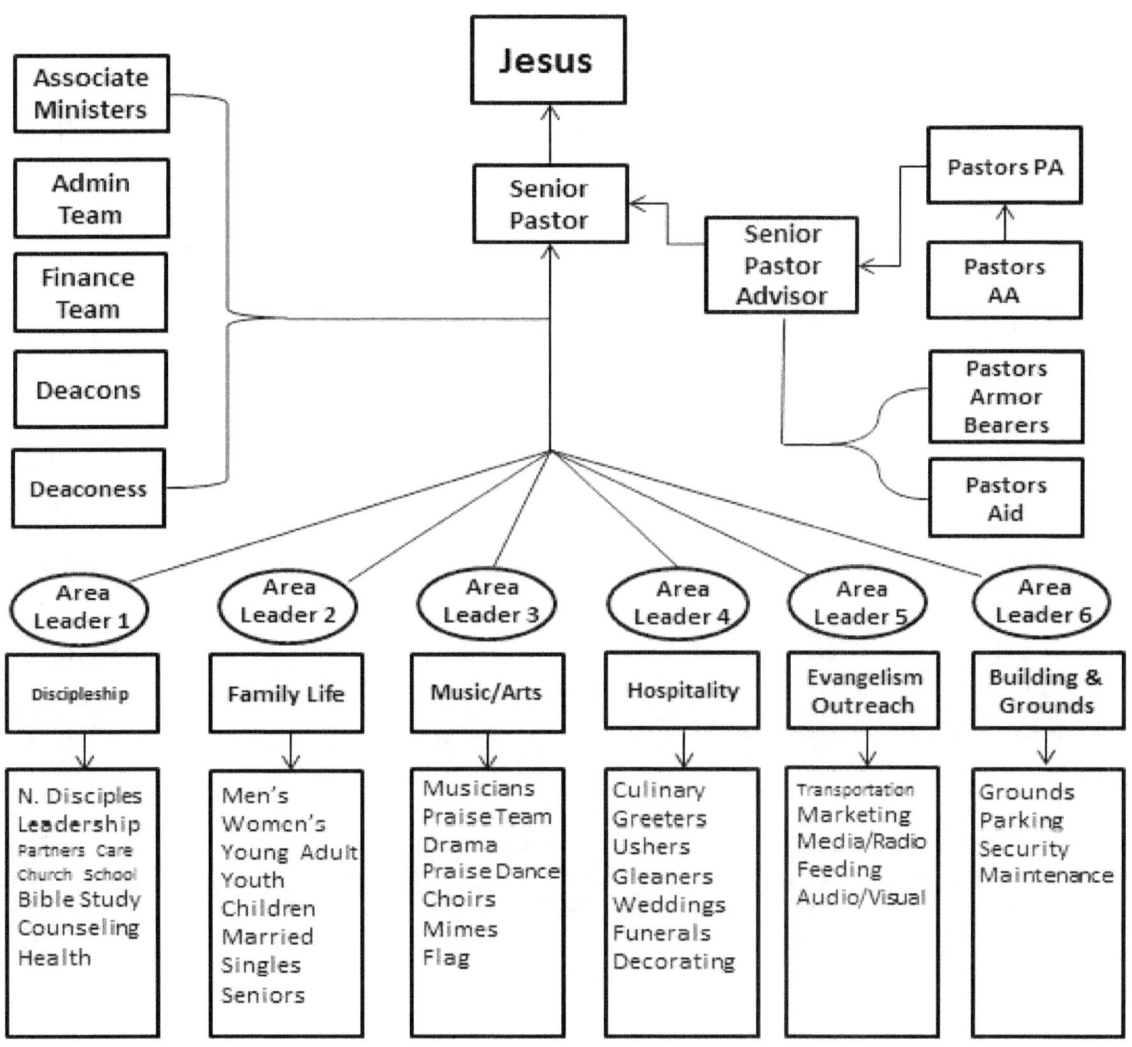

Sample Organizational Chart

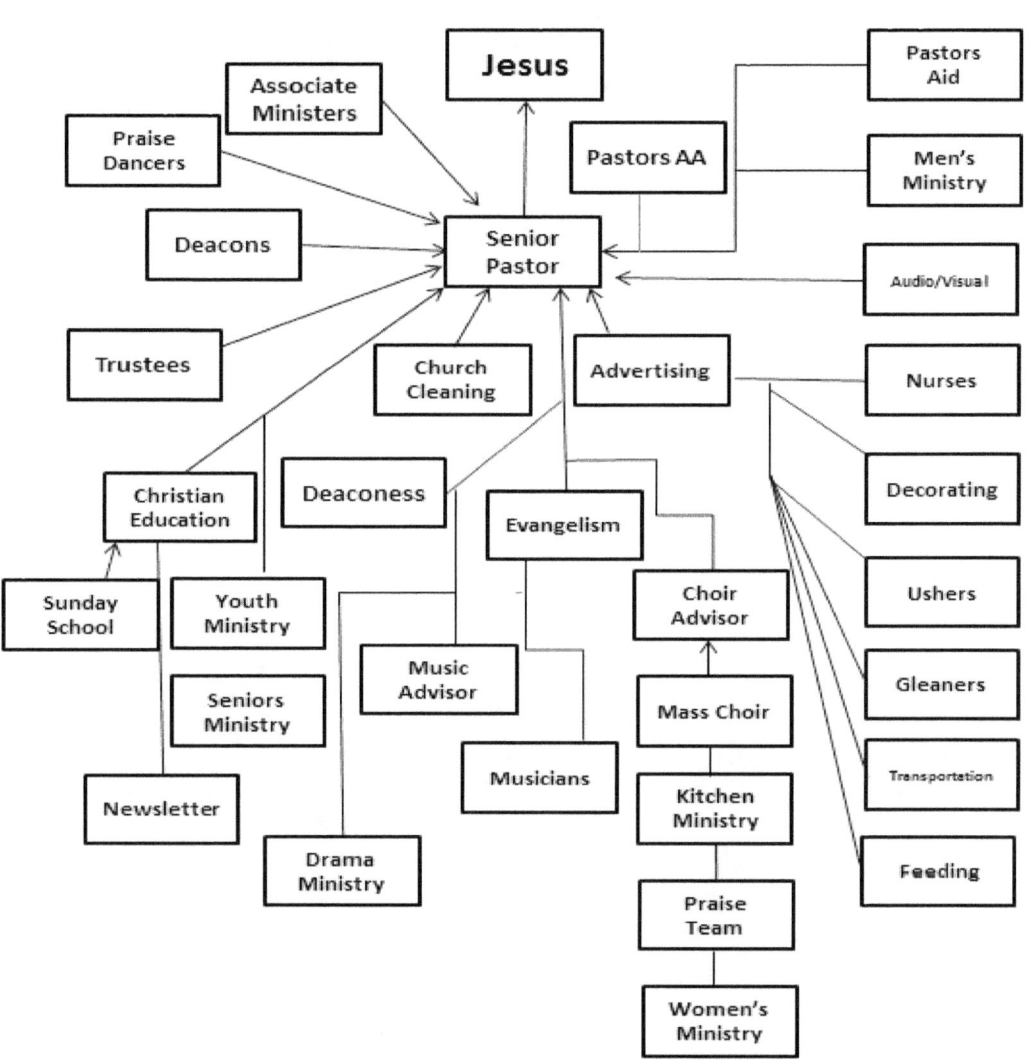

Sample Organizational Chart

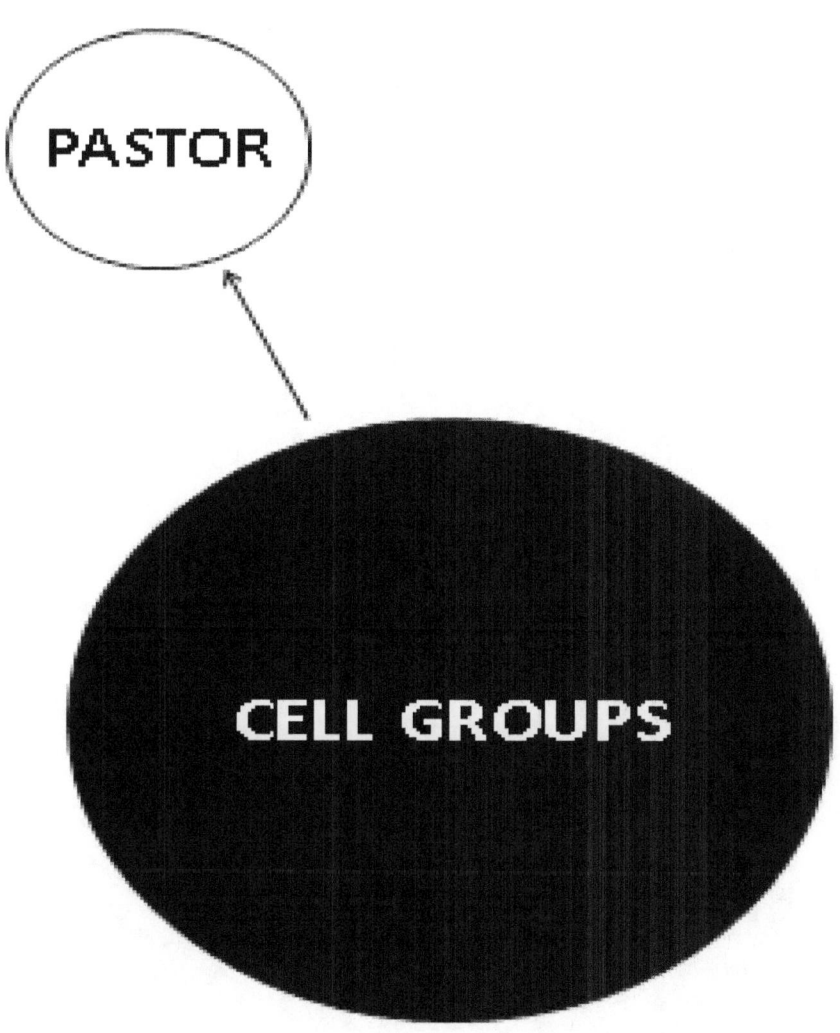

Sample Organizational Chart

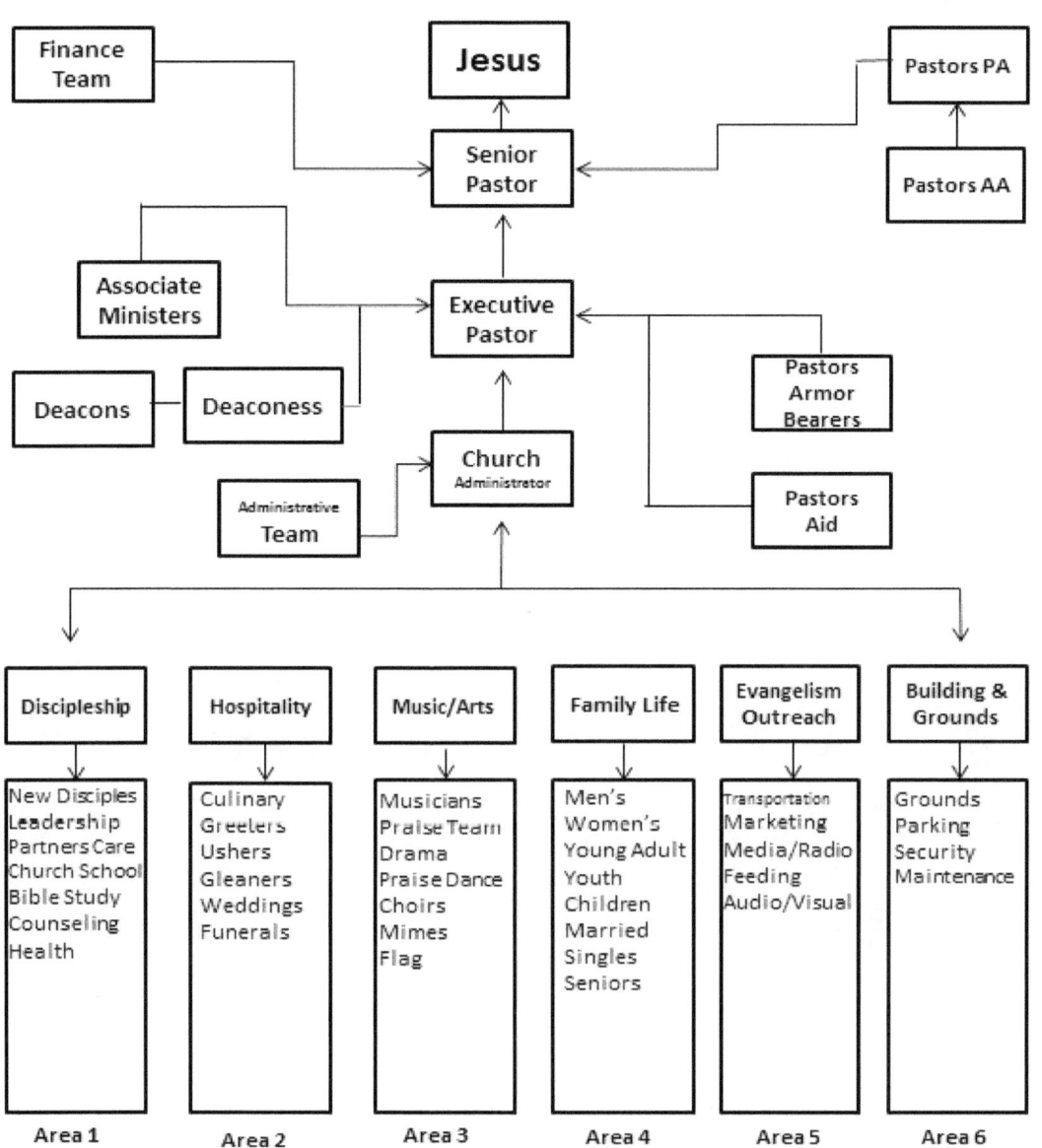

Sample Organizational Chart

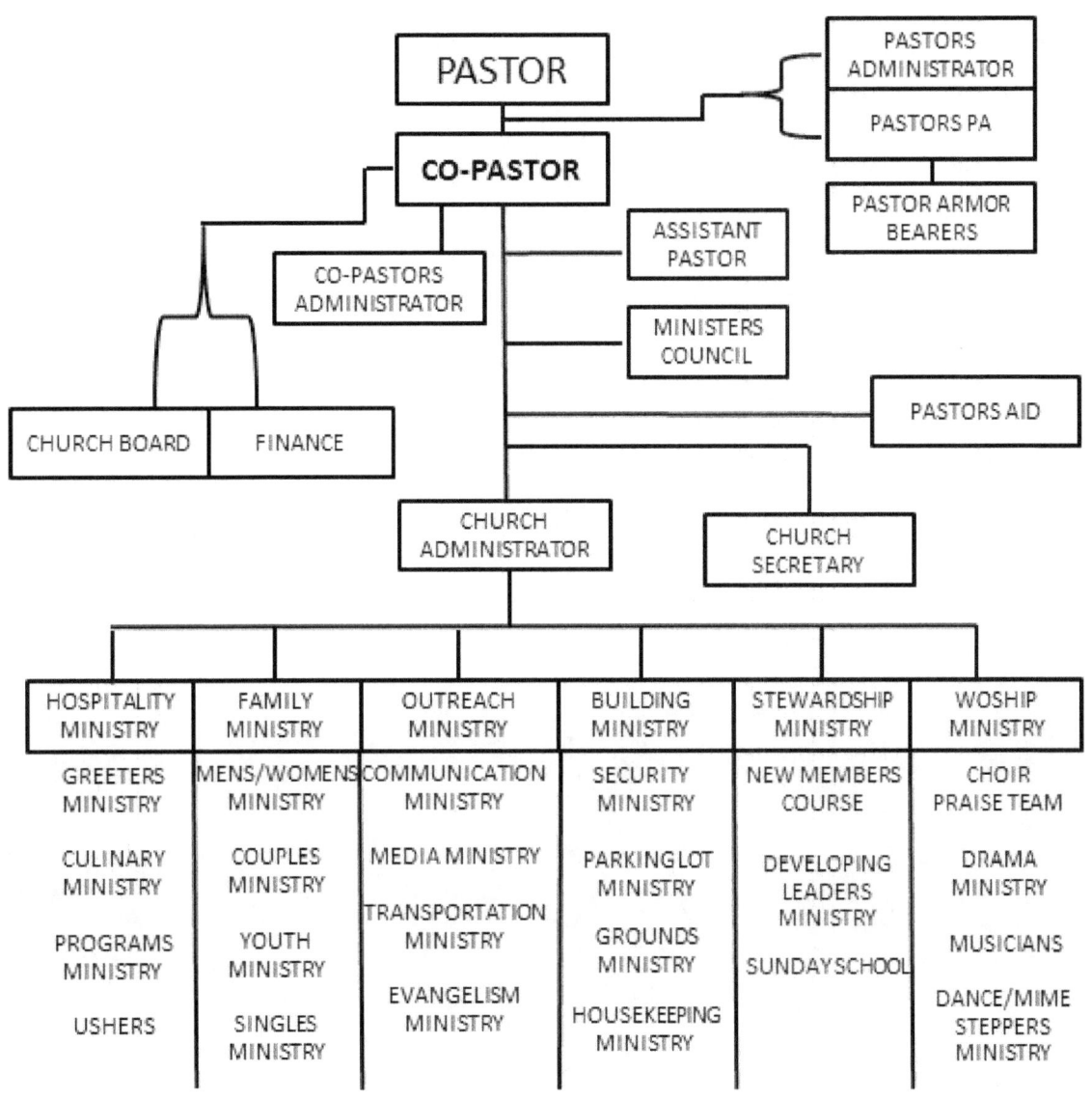

Sample Organizational Chart

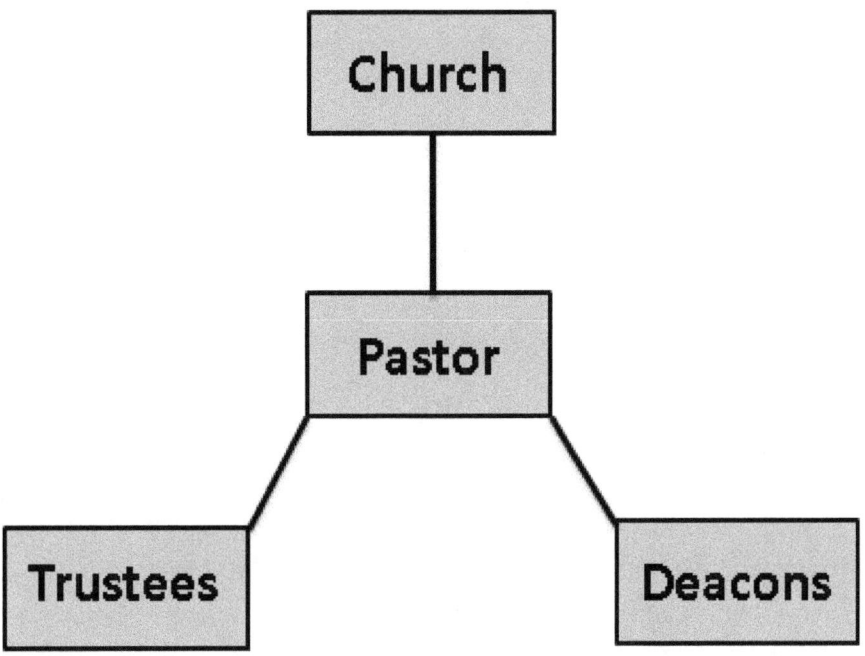

APPENDIX C
Congregational Care Organizational Chart
(Based on 400 Congregants)

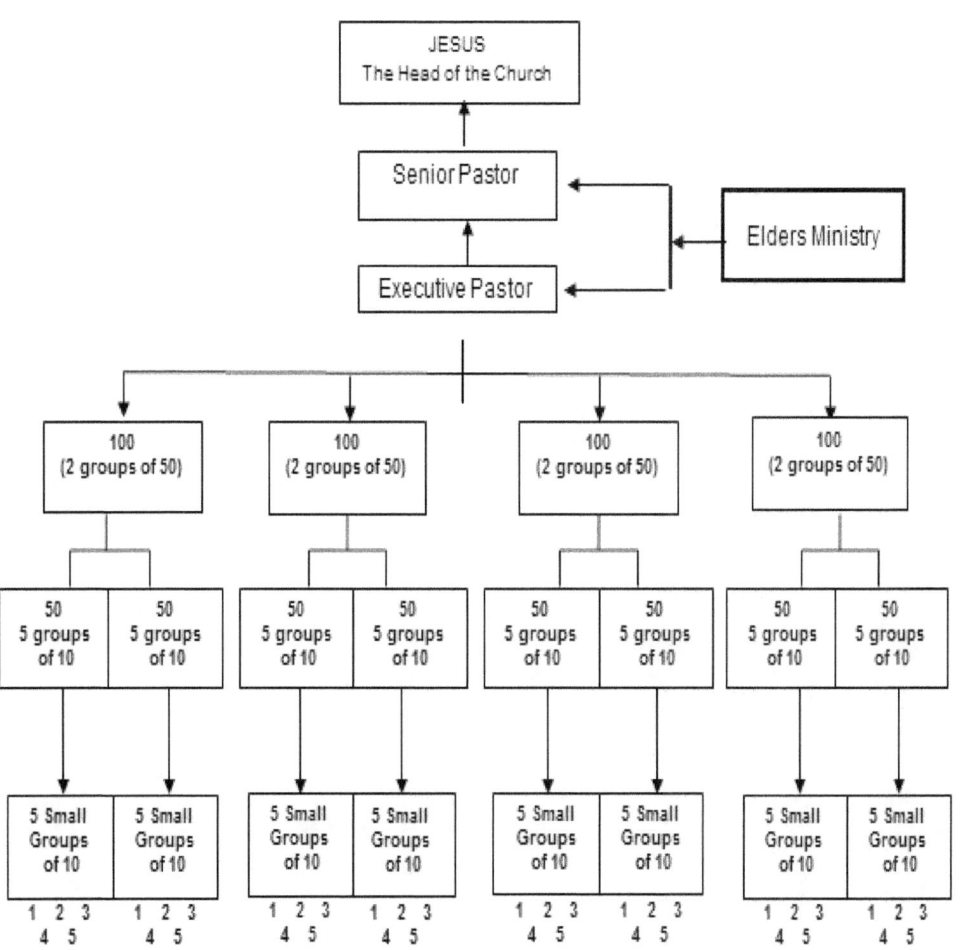

167

Equipping Spirit-Led Leaders

Empowering Current and Potential
Leaders for Kingdom Service
Workbook

TABLE OF CONTENTS

Pre-Test Questionnaire

1	Chapter 1	Leadership Foundations Discussion Question Fill In the Blank Matching
5	Chapter 2	Leading by Understanding Spiritual Gifts Multiple Guess True or False / Fill In the Blank Matching
9	Chapter 3	Leadership Roles in the Church Fill In the Blank True or False
13	Chapter 4	Leading Effectively Fill In the Blank True or False Case Studies Conflict Management Style Assessment
23	Chapter 5	Learning of Recommended Readings Multiple Guess

Answer Key

Post-Test Questionnaire

Journal

Pre-Test Questionnaire

Please Take This Pre-Test Before Starting This Workbook

Please respond to each statement below by answering the appropriate question as indicated. For each question please check the appropriate area according to the response scale below. Please provide your best answers.

Response Scale
SA = Strongly Agree; A = Agree; N = Neither Agree nor Disagree; D = Disagree; SD = Strongly Disagree

Pre-Test
There is no right or wrong answers for the Pre-Test.

Part I

UNDERSTANDING SPIRITUAL GIFTS	SA	A	N	D	SD
1. Everyone has a gift.					
2. I know the difference between motivational, manifestation, and ministry gifts.					
3. I know what my gifts are.					
4. Everyone has the same gifts.					
5. Gifts should not be used in the church.					
6. My gift has nothing to do with the ministries I enjoy.					
7. I understand why I am the way I am.					
8. My gifts are activated at 21.					
9. I am effectively using my gifts.					

Part II & Part III

UNDERSTANDING LEADERSHIP ROLES	SA	A	N	D	SD
1. Leaders should be able to train his/her team partners.					
2. Leaders are influencers.					
3. Leaders should train protégés.					
4. Leaders should encourage self-development for each team partner.					
5. The leader should spend time investing in each team partner.					
6. Leaders should desire to build character in team partners.					
7. Leaders should make changes only when the team partners are in agreement.					
8. A leader should follow-up on delegated assignments.					
9. A leader should know how to organize.					
HOW TO EFFECTIVELY LEAD	SA	A	N	D	SD
1. A leader should convey all messages in writing.					
2. Leadership requires delegation.					
3. The leader is responsible for what his/her team partners produce.					
4. It is the leader's responsibility to ensure each team partner understands the goal.					
5. The leader should receive all of the credit for fruitful progress.					
6. If it is not broken, do not be concerned with improving it.					
7. If team partners fail, leadership has failed.					
8. A leader should never admit fault.					
9. A leader has the right to speak condescendingly to his/her team partners.					

Chapter 1
Leadership Foundations

Discussion Questions

1. What are some of the issues with church leadership?

2. What is leadership?

3. Who can be a leader?

4. What are the three items listed that will empower leaders?

5. Who are Christian leaders called to influence?

6. Why are some pastors frustrated with their leaders?

7. What hinders the growth of a ministry?

8. According to the sermon, *The Skills of Leadership, Part 3*, by what two traits/qualities are leaders made?

9. Who do you respect as a quality leader? Why?

10. Explain your leadership experience.

Fill in the Blanks

1. From kings, biblical patriarchs and historical heroes there has been one consistency—_____.

2. My leaders are not committed to the tasks at hand. They are _____ and seemingly unconcerned about the church's programming.

3. Leadership is one of the _____ _____ in helping individuals to become all that _____ wants them to become.

4. If you begin right now to take a few leaders with you toward a _____ focus, then you will eventually see the results that you now label as potential.

5. _____ map out directions for others to follow as a result of their foresight.

6. Leaders are those who can _____, _____, _____, _____ and commission other individuals as well as _____ their gifts and talents for service for the Kingdom.

7. A leader is a responsible person who should take _____ when things are right or wrong.

8. It is imperative to know the type of _____ that a leader receives, especially if there is an option to choose the best _____.

9. Leadership is a function of knowing yourself, having a _____ that is well-communicated and taking effective action.

10. _____ by itself is not enough.

Matching

1. Leadership   the purpose of the church

2. Entitlement   releases, creates, about His mission

3. Pastors   map out directions for others

4. Empowerment   influencing others

5. God's heart   frustrated with leaders

6. Leaders   a church is modest/simplified/exhilarating

7. Kingdom-focus   controls, kills, about our agendas

Chapter 2
Leading by Understanding Spiritual Gifts

Multiple Guess

1. What is the Greek word for gift?
    a. Gnosis
    b. Klesis
    c. Charisma
    d. Pistis

2. Which is one of the ministry gifts?
    a. Apostle
    b. Prophecy
    c. Exhorter
    d. Giver

3. Which category of gifts is often referred to as "the five-fold ministry?"
    a. Motivational gifts
    b. Mentoring gifts
    c. Ministry gifts
    d. Manifestation gifts

4. Which is one of the motivational gifts?
    a. Evangelist
    b. Server
    c. Word of Wisdom
    d. Prophet

5. How many original apostles where there?
    a. 11
    b. 1
    c. 70
    d. 12

6. What other name is used for pastor?
    a. Ruler
    b. Overseer
    c. Administrator
    d. Prophet

7. What is the purpose of ministry gifts?
    a. To make men strong
    b. To equip & perfect the saints
    c. To make the devil mad
    d. To perfectly manipulate saints

8. Which is not a manifestation gift?
    a. Teacher
    b. Discerning of Spirits
    c. Faith
    d. Tongues

9. What motivational gift is often used by the evangelist?
    a. Giver
    b. Prophecy
    c. Helps
    d. Exhort

10. Which ministry gift nurtures the saints?
    a. Teacher
    b. Prophet
    c. Pastor
    d. Mercy

True or False

1. T___ F___ God does not want us ignorant concerning gifts.
2. T___ F___ If you prophesy you are a prophet.
3. T___ F___ If you do not use it you will lose it.
4. T___ F___ Prophets are sometimes referred to as perceivers.
5. T___ F___ Timothy and Titus were pastors.
6. T___ F___ Only women are evangelists.
7. T___ F___ God knows which gift you have before birth.
8. T___ F___ Server is diakonia in Greek.
9. T___ F___ Everyone is unique.
10. T___ F___ If you sin, you lose your gift.
11. T___ F___ Paul was a pastor.
12. T___ F___ Motivational gifts are given at the age of 12.
13. T___ F___ Jesus gave gifts to mankind.
14. T___ F___ Your pastor gives you the gifts to use for ministry.
15. T___ F___ There are no more apostles or prophets today.

Fill in the Blank

1. The _____ gifts are a category of seven gifts.
2. Spirit calls _____ for the church.
3. It was probably a main duty of the _____ to teach.
4. A higher level of authority was given to the _____ in the early church.
5. God calls leaders for His _____ which will not be self-serving to the leader.

Matching

1. Manifestation Gift   necessary to activate all the gifts

2. Prophecy   shares in a liberal manner

3. Gnosis   given much authority in the Early Church

4. Mercy   speaking forth of the mind of God

5. Ministry Gift   there are nine of them

6. Apostle   imparts the spiritual gifts by choice

7. Giver   equipped to win souls

8. Faith   encouraged Timothy & Titus

9. Holy Spirit   five-fold ministry

10. Word of Wisdom   the Greek word for knowledge

11. Charisma   supernatural insight to solve problems

12. Operations   the Greek word for teaching

13. Evangelist   also called motivational gifts

14. Paul   empathy with the misery of another

15. Didaskalia   the Greek word for gift

Chapter 3
Leadership Roles in the Church

Fill in the Blank

1. In some cases there is a _____ that presides over the appointments of leaders.

2. Yet a church cannot do its best work without _____.

3. _____ are held to a higher standard of responsibility.

4. The opposite of sound doctrine is _____ talk.

5. The _____ of biblical times became the authority in projecting the gospel and leading the flock according to sound doctrine.

6. The _____ was accountable as the general overseer in all matters of the church.

7. The _____ church is comprised of a variety of local churches with different people who congregate regularly for the purpose of teaching, fellowship, and worship.

8. The Apostle _____ was very instrumental in giving pastoral charge to specific community members.

9. There are _____, who function as pastoral assistants by also leading the church alongside the elders.

10. We ask you, _____, to respect those who labor among you, and are over you in the Lord.

True or False

1. T___ F___ Overseer and Deacon are used synonymously.
2. T___ F___ Pastors do not need to pray for their flock-they will be ok.
3. T___ F___ Paul instructed the pastors and elders what to do.
4. T___ F___ Peter trained Timothy and Titus.
5. T___ F___ Pastor is the most discussed leader in the New Testament.
6. T___ F___ Elders and shepherds teach and equip the congregation.
7. T___ F___ Leaders do not have to answer to anyone.
8. T___ F___ Titus appointed elders in Crete.
9. T___ F___ Deacons are in charge of Pastors.
10. T___ F___ Paul did not instruct leaders in Thessalonica.
11. T___ F___ There are no biblical qualifications to be a deacon.
12. T___ F___ Paul sent Timothy to Ephesus.
13. T___ F___ Barnabas was not an apostle.
14. T___ F___ Leaders empower their brothers and sisters to seek God.
15. T___ F___ Bishops were assisted by presbyters.
16. T___ F___ Deacons supervise the work of the bishop.
17. T___ F___ Good character is one of the qualifications of a deacon.
18. T___ F___ Church officers such as trustees are acquired out of necessity.
19. T___ F___ All church leaders are Christians.
20. T___ F___ Paul is the head of the body of Christ.
21. T___ F___ Pastors should protect their sheep.
22. T___ F___ Church leaders should be followers of Jesus.
23. T___ F___ Having business skills outweighs spiritual behavior.
24. T___ F___ Church leaders are immune to corruption.
25. T___ F___ Wolves are sent by satan to lead people astray.

Discussion Questions

1. According to Acts 14:22, who was appointed to the local church?

2. What was the structure of the church according to Philippians 1:1?

3. Of what is the Universal church comprised?

4. What were the two offices recognized in the church by the time the Pastoral Epistles were written?

5. In your own words compare the following: the biblical role of the pastor vs the contemporary role of the pastor.

Chapter 4
Leading Effectively

Fill in the Blank

1. The medium for spiritual _____ is prayer to God in order to receive directions for the empowerment of the masses.

2. Pastors should _____ for their members, parents for their children, and leaders for those they lead.

3. It is imperative that God's leaders develop a life of _____ and spiritual discipline.

4. One can employ _____ _____ in a secular environment; however, _____ _____ cannot always be employed in a spiritual environment.

5. The apostles devoted themselves _____ to prayer, and to the _____ of the word.

6. The preacher has an _____ to travail in prayer in private to ask God to protect the Word in the hearts of the hearer in order to bear fruit to God's eternal _____.

7. _____ is a conversation with God on the behalf of others and self.

8. When we pray, we pray with the _____ of receiving in faith, believing it is done.

9. _____ leads to the growth in trust and confidence.

10. It will be difficult to lead _____ without a commitment to prayer.

True or False

1. T___ F___ Prayer is important to the life of a leader.
2. T___ F___ We often pray when things are going wrong.
3. T___ F___ Petitioning means giving thanks.
4. T___ F___ Prayer is a waste of time.
5. T___ F___ No faith is needed when praying to God.
6. T___ F___ We pray with the purpose of receiving in faith.
7. T___ F___ Men should always pray and not faint.
8. T___ F___ Pleading is tailoring the prayer to the need.
9. T___ F___ Prayer is an essential part of a believer's spiritual defense.
10. T___ F___ God will never answer prayer on Wednesdays.
11. T___ F___ God communicates with his Leaders through prayer.
12. T___ F___ Prayer does not change anything in the natural realm.
13. T___ F___ Praising means making a request to God.
14. T___ F___ Leaders at Colossae were always praying for their people.
15. T___ F___ Paul did not care much for prayer.
16. T___ F___ Prayer brings fulfillment that one can find empowerment.
17. T___ F___ Jesus isolated Himself often just to pray.
18. T___ F___ When we pray there is no one there to answer.
19. T___ F___ Jesus is mankind's connector to God.
20. T___ F___ Prayer and the Word of God do not go together.
21. T___ F___ The result of prayer is transformative.
22. T___ F___ Martin Luther did not believe in prayer.
23. T___ F___ God does not want our hearts and minds tuned into Him.
24. T___ F___ Personalizing is beseeching God on the behalf of others.
25. T___ F___ Leaders should desire what God desires.

Conflict Resolution and The Leader: Case Studies

Read the case studies below answer the questions and determine a biblical resolution that would diffuse the problem and/or reconcile the parties involved.

1. You have been the chairman of deacons in your church for over twelve years and you love your pastor and church. One day you find out that the pastor was caught up in a questionable situation which is later confirmed true. There are some in leadership who want to fire the pastor, some want to keep him and others are leaving because of the negative aftermath. The pastor wants to ask the church to forgive him so that he could stay.

   Who will be affected by your decision?
   If you were the pastor, how would you want to be treated?
   How important is this situation anyway?

2. You just joined a ministry five weeks ago. The first four weeks were full of excitement and you felt that you made the right decision. However after the fourth week, you were approached by two longtime members who began to adversely talk about the leadership in the church. You start to feel uncomfortable with the conversation but they continued to get deeper and more belligerent concerning how they feel about leadership.

   How do you turn this conversation into a positive one?
   How will you relate to the two longtime members in the future?
   As a new member, how does this make you feel about the leadership?

3. You are longtime friends with one of the members on the finance ministry of your church. One evening the two of you go out for dinner at an expensive restaurant and have a wonderful time. When it is time to pay the check your friend says that they will pay for it and pulls out the credit card that belongs to the church to do so. You are concerned about it so you speak up. They tell you that it is okay because they do it all the time. Plus they tell you that the church has plenty of money, and they will never miss it.

    Should anyone else get involved? If so, who and/or why?
    How will your friendship be affected by your decision?
    What message does this convey about your friend's leadership?

4. You are the coordinator of the choir. One evening at choir rehearsal you walk in on the minister of music and one of the leaders of the church who are involved in a rather obvious intimate exchange. They are both married to two other leaders of the church, who are down the hall in a youth meeting. They both say to you it is not what you think and ask if you would keep quiet about what you saw.

    What would be your next comment?
    Should anyone else get involved? If so, who and/or why?
    How can you turn this situation into a positive one?

5. You are asked to be the chairperson of a committee in the church and you accept the invitation. Later you find out that the co-chairperson with whom you will have to work is someone who does not favor you and has undermined your decisions in the past. In addition, she has not spoken to you in five years because of how she personally feels about you.

   How can you make this a win-win situation for all?
   Is any response necessary? If so, how long will it take you to respond?
   How does this affect you spiritually as a leader?

6. A new convert joined the church that you attend approximately a month ago. The superintendent of Church school asked the new convert, who happens to be his boss, to teach a class. There was no objection by the leadership because they said that there was no one else who will teach. When you attend the class you discover that the new convert neither knows how to teach nor familiar with the Bible. As a matter of fact, the new convert often asks others in the class for their thoughts because he does not know how to teach. He refuses to stop teaching the class because he likes the attention.

   What would be your response at the end of the class?
   How can you make this situation work for everyone?
   What should the leadership do?

Conflict Management Style Assessment

We each have our own way of dealing with conflict. The techniques we use are based on many variables such as our basic underlying temperament, our personality, our environment and where we are in our professional career. However, by and large there are five major styles of conflict management techniques in our tool box. In order to address conflict we draw from a collaborating, competing, avoiding, harmonizing or compromising style of management. None of these strategies is superior in and of itself. How effective they are depends on the context in which they are used.

Each statement below provides a strategy for dealing with a conflict. Rate each statement by circling a number on a scale of 1 to 4 indicating how likely you are to use this strategy. Be sure to answer the questions indicating how you would behave rather than how you think you should behave.

1. I explore issues with others so as to find solutions that meet everyone's needs.

    1 = Rarely; 2 = Sometimes; 3 = Often; 4 = Always

2. I try to negotiate and adopt a give-and-take approach to problem situations

    1 = Rarely; 2 = Sometimes; 3 = Often; 4 = Always

3. I try to meet the expectations of others.

    1 = Rarely; 2 = Sometimes; 3 = Often; 4 = Always

4. I would argue my case and insist on the merits of my point of view.

    1= Rarely; 2 = Sometimes; 3 = Often; 4 = Always

5. When there is a disagreement, I gather as much information as I can and keep the lines of communication open.

    1 = Rarely; 2 = Sometimes; 3 = Often; 4 = Always

6. When I find myself in an argument, I usually say very little and try to leave as soon as possible.

    1 = Rarely; 2 = Sometimes; 3 = Often; 4 = Always

7. I try to see conflicts from both sides. What do I need? What does the other person need? What are the issues involved?

    1 = Rarely; 2 = Sometimes; 3 = Often; 4 = Always

8. I prefer to compromise when solving problems and just move on.

    1 = Rarely; 2 = Sometimes; 3 = Often; 4 = Always

9. I find conflicts challenging and exhilarating; I enjoy the battle of wits that usually follows.

    1 = Rarely; 2 = Sometimes; 3 = Often; 4 = Always

10. Being at odds with other people makes me feel uncomfortable and anxious.

    1 = Rarely; 2 = Sometimes; 3 = Often; 4 = Always

11. I try to accommodate the wishes of my friends and family.

    1 = Rarely; 2 = Sometimes; 3 = Often; 4 = Always

12. I can figure out what needs to be done and I am usually right.

    1 = Rarely; 2 = Sometimes; 3 = Often; 4 = Always

13. To break deadlocks, I would meet people halfway.

    1 = Rarely; 2 = Sometimes; 3 = Often; 4 = Always

14. I may not get what I want but it's a small price to pay for keeping the peace.

    1 = Rarely; 2 = Sometimes; 3 = Often; 4 = Always

15. I avoid hard feelings by keeping my disagreements with others to myself.

    1 = Rarely; 2 = Sometimes; 3 = Often; 4 = Always

How to Score the Conflict Management Quiz

As stated, the 15 statements correspond to the five conflict resolution styles. To find your most preferred style, total the points in the respective categories. The one with the highest score indicates your most used strategy. The one with the lowest score indicates your least used strategy. However, if you are a leader who must deal with conflict regularly, you may find your style to be a blend of styles.

Style Corresponding Statements: Total

Collaborating: #1, #5, #7   Competing: #4, #9, #12   Avoiding: #6, #10, #15
Harmonizing: #3, #11, #14   Compromising: #2, #8, #13

Collaborating Style: Problems are solved to achieve an optimum result for all involved. Both sides get what they want and negative feelings are minimized.
Pros: Creates mutual trust; maintains positive relationships; builds commitments.
Cons: Time consuming; energy consuming.

Competing Style: Authoritarian approach.
Pros: Goal oriented; quick.
Cons: May breed hostility.

Avoiding Style: The non-confrontational approach.
Pros: Does not escalate conflict; postpones difficulty.
Cons: Unaddressed problems; unresolved problems.

Harmonizing Style: Giving in to maintain relationships.
Pros: Minimizes injury when we are outmatched; relationships are maintained.
Cons: Breeds resentment; exploits the weak.

Compromising Style: The middle ground approach.
Pros: Useful in complex issues without simple solutions; all parties are equal in power.
Cons: No one is ever really satisfied; less than optimal solutions get implemented.[186]

---

[186] Reginald Adkins, Elemental Truths, http://www.ncsu.edu/grad/preparing-future leaders/docs/conflict-management-styles-quiz.pdf (accessed August 1, 2012).

Chapter 5
Learning of Recommended Readings

Multiple Guess

1. It explains that individuals have a desire to communicate with God even if there is not a belief that God will answer.
    a. Life With God: Reading The Bible For Spiritual Transformation
    b. The Art Of Prayer: A Simple Guide To Conversation With God
    c. Josephus: The Essential Writings
    d. Introductory Lectures in Systematic Theology

2. It encourages creative thinking and new ways of achieving a positive result.
    a. The Soul of Leadership
    b. Leadership Secrets from the Bible
    c. Life With God: Reading The Bible For Spiritual Transformation
    d. Organizing Genius: The Secret of Creative Collaboration

3. Prayer is defined as a gift from God for the body of Christ and designed to bring one closer to God through this familiar line of communication.
    a. The Power of Prayer in a Believer's Life
    b. Prayers Ancient and Modern
    c. Let Us Pray
    d. Cultivating The Discipline Of Prayer: The Key To Having Power With God

4. It shares how-to methods of handling conflict and stressful situations with flair and professionalism.
    a. I Believe in the Holy Spirit
    b. The Pulpit Commentary
    c. Dealing with Difficult
    d. Christian Theology

Post-Test Questionnaire

Please Take This Post-Test After Finishing This Workbook

Please respond to each statement below by answering the appropriate question as indicated. For each question please check the appropriate area according to the response scale below. Please provide your best answers.

Response Scale

SA = Strongly Agree; A = Agree; N = Neither Agree nor Disagree; D = Disagree; SD = Strongly Disagree

Post-Test

There is no right or wrong answers for the Post-Test.

Part I

UNDERSTANDING SPIRITUAL GIFTS	SA	A	N	D	SD
1. Everyone has a gift.					
2. I know the difference between motivational, manifestation, and ministry gifts.					
3. I know what my gifts are.					
4. Everyone has the same gifts.					
5. Gifts should not be used in the church.					
6. My gift has nothing to do with the ministries I enjoy.					
7. I understand why I am the way I am.					
8. My gifts are activated at 21.					
9. I am effectively using my gifts.					

Part II & Part III

UNDERSTANDING LEADERSHIP ROLES	SA	A	N	D	SD
1. Leaders should be able to train his/her team partners.					
2. Leaders are influencers.					
3. Leaders should train protégés.					
4. Leaders should encourage self-development for each team partner.					
5. The leader should spend time investing in each team partner.					
6. Leaders should desire to build character in team partners.					
7. Leaders should make changes only when the team partners are in agreement.					
8. A leader should follow-up on delegated assignments.					
9. A leader should know how to organize.					
HOW TO EFFECTIVELY LEAD	SA	A	N	D	SD
1. A leader should convey all messages in writing.					
2. Leadership requires delegation.					
3. The leader is responsible for what his/her team partners produce.					
4. It is the leader's responsibility to ensure each team partner understands the goal.					
5. The leader should receive all of the credit for fruitful progress.					
6. If it is not broken, do not be concerned with improving it.					
7. If team partners fail, leadership has failed.					
8. A leader should never admit fault.					
9. A leader has the right to speak condescendingly to his/her team partners.					

You may notice a change in your Post-Test answers as a result of finishing this study. This is designed to reduce the selection of neutral and to foster the choice of a more definitive answer.

ANSWER KEY

Answer Key for Chapter 1

Chapter 1
Discussion Questions
1. Lack of training; do not want change; Entitlement Mentality
2. Influence
3. Any can be a leader
4. Understanding spiritual gifts; the roles in the church and how to effectively lead
5. The world
6. They don't show up for training; no motivation; stuck
7. Avoidance of training
8. Choices & Circumstances
9. Your answer
10. Your answer

Chapter 1
Fill in the Blank
1. Leadership
2. Unmotivated
3. Key essentials; God
4. Kingdom
5. Leaders
6. Develop, Lead, Mentor, Train
7. Responsibility
8. Teaching; Leader
9. Vision
10. Influence

Chapter 1
Matching

Leadership	influencing others
Entitlement	controls, kills, about our agendas
Pastors	frustrated with leaders
Empowerment	releases, creates, about His mission
God's heart	the purpose of the church
Leaders	map out directions for others
Kingdom-focus	a church is modest/simplified/exhilarating

Answer Key for Chapter 2

Chapter 2
Multiple Guess

1. C   6. B
2. A   7. B
3. C   8. A
4. B   9. D
5. D   10. C

Chapter 2
True or False

1. T   6. F   11. F
2. F   7. T   12. F
3. F   8. T   13. T
4. T   9. T   14. F
5. T   10. F   15. F

Chapter 2
Fill in the Blank

1. Motivational
2. Leaders
3. Pastor
4. Apostle
5. Purpose

Chapter 2
Matching

1. Manifestation Gifts — there are nine of them
2. Prophecy — speaking forth of the mind and counsel of God
3. Gnosis — the Greek word for knowledge
4. Mercy — empathy with the misery of another
5. Ministry Gifts — five-fold ministry
6. Apostle — given much authority in the Early Church
7. Giver — shares in a liberal manner
8. Faith — necessary to activate all the gifts
9. Holy Spirit — imparts the spiritual gifts by choice
10. Word of Wisdom — supernatural insight to solve problems
11. Charisma — the Greek word for gift
12. Operation — also called motivational gifts
13. Evangelist — equipped to win souls
14. Paul — encouraged Timothy & Titus
15. Didaskalia — the Greek word for teaching

Answer Key for Chapter 3

Chapter 3
Fill in the Blank
1. Bishop
2. Officers
3. Leaders
4. Meaningless
5. Evangelist
6. Bishop
7. Universal
8. Paul
9. Deacons
10. Brothers

Chapter 3
True or False
1. F	11. F	21. T
2. F	12. T	22. T
3. T	13. F	23. F
4. F	14. T	24. F
5. T	15. T	25. T
6. T	16. F	
7. F	17. T	
8. T	18. T	
9. F	19. F	
10. F	20. F	

Chapter 3
Discussion Questions
1. presbyters were appointed to leadership in every local church
2. deacons, elders and church members
3. a variety of local churches with different people who congregate regularly for the purpose of teaching, fellowship, and worship
4. Overseer; Deacon
5. Your Answer

Answer Key for Chapter 4

Chapter 4
Fill in the Blanks
1. Communication
2. Pray
3. Consecration
4. Spiritual leadership; Secular leadership
5. Continually; ministry
6. Obligation; praise
7. Prayer
8. Purpose
9. Prayer
10. Effectively

Chapter 4
True or False
1. T   11. T   21. T
2. T   12. F   22. F
3. F   13. F   23. F
4. F   14. T   24. F
5. F   15. F   25. T
6. T   16. T
7. T   17. T
8. F   18. F
9. T   19. T
10. F 20. F

Chapter 4
Case Studies
There are no wrong answers. However, a positive resolution is sought after for each situation. Consider the Scriptures below.
1. Matthew 6:14-15
2. Matthew 12:36
3. Ephesians 4:28
4. 1 Corinthians 5
5. Romans 12:17-21
6. 1 Timothy 5:21-22

Chapter 4
Conflict Management Assessment
There are no wrong answers. This section is strictly based on the individual who is taking the assessment.

Answer Key for Chapter 5

Chapter 5
Multiple Guess
1. B
2. D
3. C
4. C

Order Information

To contact Dr. Perkins for
speaking engagements, visit the website at:

ItsmeDrIFP.org

You may also order paperback books,
sow seeds and/or view itinerary
at the above website.

Please email: (itsmeDrIP@aol.com)
or call for bulk orders

Like our page on Facebook at: Itsme-Dr Ifp

Follow us on Twitter: @itsmeDrIFP

Mailing Address is:

Dr. I. Franklin Perkins
P.O. Box 9523
Hampton, VA 23670
757-825-0030